The Dissertation & the Discipline

Also in the CrossCurrents series

Attending to the Margins
Writing, Researching, and Teaching on the Front Lines

Coming of Age
The Advanced Writing Curriculum

Coming to Class
Pedagogy and the Social Class of Teachers

Composition, Pedagogy, and the Scholarship of Teaching

The Dissertation & the Discipline
Reinventing Composition Studies

Feminist Empirical Research
Emerging Perspectives on Qualitative and Teacher Research

Foregrounding Ethical Awareness in Composition and English Studies

Getting Restless
Rethinking Revision in Writing Instruction

Good Intentions
Writing Center Work for Postmodern Times

Grading in the Post-Process Classroom
From Theory to Practice

Gypsy Academics and Mother-Teachers
Gender, Contingent Labor, and Writing Instruction

Kitchen Cooks, Plate Twirlers, and Troubadours
Writing Program Administrators Tell Their Stories

Know and Tell
A Writing Pedagogy of Disclosure, Genre, and Membership

Life-Affirming Acts

Miss Grundy Doesn't Teach Here Anymore
Popular Culture and the Composition Classroom

The Mythology of Voice

Outbursts in Academe
Multiculturalism and Other Sources of Conflict

The Politics of Writing Centers

Race, Rhetoric, and Composition

Resituating Writing
Constructing and Administering Writing Programs

Textual Orientations
Lesbian and Gay Students and the Making of Discourse Communities

Writing in an Alien World
Basic Writing and the Struggle for Equality in Higher Education

The Dissertation & the Discipline

Reinventing Composition Studies

Edited by

Nancy Welch
Catherine G. Latterell
Cindy Moore
Sheila Carter-Tod

New Perspectives in Rhetoric and Composition

CHARLES I. SCHUSTER, SERIES EDITOR

Boynton/Cook Publishers
HEINEMANN
Portsmouth, NH

Boynton/Cook Publishers, Inc.
A subsidiary of Reed Elsevier, Inc.
361 Hanover Street
Portsmouth, NH 03801–3912
www.boyntoncook.com

Offices and agents throughout the world

Library of Congress Cataloging-in-Publication Data
The dissertation & the discipline : reinventing composition studies / edited by Nancy Welch . . . [et al.].
p. cm.—(CrossCurrents)
Includes bibliographical references.
ISBN 0-86709-520-2 (pbk. : alk. paper)
1. Dissertations, Academic—United States. 2. Academic writing—United States. 3. English language—Rhetoric–Study and teaching—United States. I. Welch, Nancy, 1963– II. CrossCurrents (Portsmouth, N.H.)
LB2369 .D46 2002
808'.02—dc21
2002005831

Editor: Charles Schuster
Production service: Kim Arney Mulcahy
Production coordinator: Lynne Reed
Cover design: Jenny Jensen Greenleaf
Cover illustration: "The Natural," by Michael Smith
Typesetter: Kim Arney Mulcahy
Manufacturing: Steve Bernier

Printed in the United States of America on acid-free paper
06 05 04 03 02 VP 1 2 3 4 5

Contents

Introduction

At a recent conference, during a lively panel on feminist pragmatic action, a doctoral candidate announced that she would be defending her dissertation that very afternoon. The large audience of established scholars, recent PhDs, and graduate students burst into applause. Then the candidate added, her tone turning regretful, that of course she'd had to write her dissertation in a traditional fashion—the lit review/three examples/conclusion form that's as familiar to dissertators as the five-paragraph theme once was to undergraduates. All cheeriness exited the room. No one spoke. No one said anything about feminist action. All seemed agreed that the state of the dissertation in composition and rhetoric could be lamented but not changed.

The Dissertation and the Discipline: Reinventing Composition Studies intervenes in this discipline-wide silence surrounding the dissertation. Contributors come from a range of institutional and social contexts. Several drafted their chapters while drafting their own dissertations. Others speak from years of directing graduate students. All are joined in the belief that we face an urgent task: to provide all participants in doctoral programs with the means to talk publicly and productively about the dissertation *as* a rhetorical situation, as a culturally engaged scene of writing that can be examined, questioned, and revised.

This task shouldn't be so difficult. Philosophical orientations and program particulars notwithstanding, compositionists are trained to approach undergraduate writing pedagogy in the spirit of critique and possibility. Yet, curiously, this spirit has not been brought to bear on the penultimate writing assignment marking the transition from student to professional. "The purpose of the dissertation is to demonstrate mastery of the field." "The purpose of the dissertation is to get a needed book publication." "The purpose of the dissertation is to just get it done." Such conflicting dissertation truisms circulate in faculty offices, graduate student lounges, and conference ballrooms, defining the dissertation without being subject to scrutiny. In present circumstances, such questions as "Why write a dissertation?" and "What can a dissertation be?" aren't heard as the start of rhetorical inquiry but instead as personal complaint or naïve wishfulness.

The Dissertation and the Discipline seeks to empower both dissertation writers and their committees to hear each other's voices differently—to locate their hopes and their frustrations within the field's debates about authorship and authority, form and function, tradition and challenge. We aim for more, though, than simply extending to the dissertation the same attention paid to undergraduate writing because there's a deeper symbiosis between the dissertation and our profession, one dramatized in the anecdote of scholar-activists announcing their commitment to feminist action while renouncing their ability to change the dissertations they write and direct. When compositionists renounce their ability to change the dissertation, they renounce their ability to change the field because it's there that the field is reproduced, there that we find our most profound, persistent beliefs about what it means to write and teach. If we want to change how writing gets carried out in school, if we want our discipline to resist replicating the status quo, we need see the dissertation as a site where the discipline is not just reproduced but could be reinvented.

We are grateful to Boynton/Cook editor Lisa Luedeke, who believed that arguments for disciplinary change could and should come from dissertators and new PhDs as much as from established scholars. We're grateful as well to CrossCurrents series editor Chuck Schuster who urged us to make this a book that would not only challenge the field but challenge him, as someone who routinely directs dissertations. We'd also like to thank Marilyn Cooper for including in *College Composition and Communication* a preview of this collection's concerns (Dissertation Consortium 2001). But especially, we need to thank our contributors, who revised and revised and revised just one more time. Because of their commitment, this collection has become more varied and more contentious.

Listening to the experiences and arguments gathered here, we have to say, is hard. The dissertation may be a rhetorical scene that speaks from and to field-wide issues, but dissertation relationships are nonetheless felt as deeply personal, creating anxiety and defensiveness about public renderings. Some anonymous reviewers responded warmly to those chapters that appeared distant from a particular dissertating scene and bristled at chapters that highlight conflict, confusion, and outright pain. Other reviewers recommended that we populate the book with even more personal narratives, airing what's been kept too long under wraps. In the end, we felt that the collection needs both: chapters that render a particular moment in time and chapters that assess the broader forces of conservatism and change at work in credentialing doctoral students. As a result, the chapters complement, complicate, and sometimes counter one another.

It's true that this contentious approach—each chapter's perspectives and solutions being potentially arguable—doesn't offer the uniformity of a single-authored argument. It's also true, however, that top-down calls for dissertation reform have failed to effect change. We need to take our cue from composition's best research practices—that is, start with the messy details, attend to the contradictions of context, and learn from particular writers in particular places what the dissertation is, whose intentions it serves, and what futures doctoral students and their advisors can start to compose.

Chapter One

Writing Selves, Establishing Academic Identity

Marilyn Vogler Urion

> *The symbolic efficacy of words is exercised only in so far as the person subjected to it recognizes the person who exercises it as authorized to do so, or, what amounts to the same thing, only in so far as he [sic] fails to realize that, in submitting to it, he himself has contributed, through his recognition, to its establishment.*
>
> —Pierre Bourdieu (1991), *Language and Symbolic Power*

Many of us encourage and engage in innovative academic writing both before and after the dissertation, from the essays of first-year writing students to those of established scholars. By contrast, it is generally accepted that dissertations must adhere to narrowly conceived notions of academic discourse and to rigid formatting requirements. Understanding why this is so—how the dissertation process serves not only as demonstration that we are able to do the work of scholars but as a rite of initiation—provides insight into why the academic community is as it is and how it might become more open to diversity. As each of us goes through the process, submits to the requirements, and adheres to the guidelines, two things happen: The structure of the genre is reaffirmed and we are changed. Much about the process is consistent with Arnold van Gennep's (1908) model of initiation rites characterized by a three-stage pattern of separation, transition, and incorporation.[1]

Though we talk casually about the dissertation as a ritual of initiation, ritual is not generally thought of as its primary function. Nor do we talk seriously about the ritual aspects of measured margins, third-person pronouns, double-spacing, and standard written English. Such requirements, however, reveal the underlying ritual like old tombstones yielding their inscriptions to the rubbing of crayon on paper. Pierre Bourdieu, recognizing their social function, chooses to call initiation rituals "rites of institution" (1991, 117). Investiture, he explains, both transforms expectations persons have of those invested and ". . . simultaneously transforms the representation that the invested person has of himself, and the behavior he feels obliged to adopt in order to conform to that representation" (119). Writing a dissertation, in other words, obliges us to adopt a new set of behaviors.

Equally useful in understanding why dissertations are the way they are is Lorraine Code's (1995) notion of rhetorical spaces, spaces in which "subjectivities are variously enacted, and identities are . . . continually reconstructed in the enactings"—spaces characterized by uneven distributions of knowledge and authority. She explains:

> Rhetorical spaces, as I conceive of them here, are fictive but not fanciful or fixed locations, whose (tacit, rarely spoken) territorial imperatives structure and limit the kinds of utterances that can be voiced within them with a reasonable expectation of uptake and "choral support"; an expectation of being heard, understood, taken seriously. (ix–x)

Negotiating a voice that is acceptably within the confines of the space, one that will be "taken seriously," while at the same time maintaining fidelity to a sense of personal identity during a transforming ritual of initiation seems more difficult as a person's distance from the center of academic culture increases. Code and van Gennep show us why.

Listening to dissertation stories can also help us understand how the experience changes those who go through it and thus how the academic community is itself perpetuated. This chapter draws on dissertation stories I gathered during my own initiation into academe.[2] Though participants didn't talk about being engaged in an initiation ritual, as I listened to their stories, I saw patterns emerge that were consistent with van Gennep's model. Similarly, characteristics of the rhetorical spaces that Code describes are openly apparent in dissertation stories. I heard stories of persons being told to set aside projects they wanted to work on in favor of something more "appropriate." I consistently heard stories of giving in to revision demands that ranged from conceptual restructuring to the use of the word *that*. At the same time, people shared stories of supportive friends, advisors, and committees. Supportive advisors, in fact, seem to be the rule, a phenomenon consistent with initiation rituals where a guide both tests and protects the initiate.

Supportive advisors, however, do not mitigate the fundamental role that rites of initiation play in maintaining institutional uniformity. The rhetorical space of dissertations remains conservative in that it (1) adheres to particular hierarchies of power and privilege and (2) relies on a particular distribution of knowledge and authority, both of which maintain dominant culture privilege in the academy. Advisors and committees, as well as students, are constrained by the conventions of this space. That these constraints are shared explains, perhaps, the general feeling of a diminishing space for risk-taking. At the prospectus stage, constraints may mean being realistic about what can be accomplished. Later, concerns about the public reception of the work appear. The advisor of one dissertator in my study, for instance, expressed concern late in the process that risks a student takes may reflect badly on the student's advisor and department, illustrating Bourdieu's claim that "the function of all magical boundaries [is] to stop those who are inside, on the right side of the line, from leaving, demeaning, or down-grading themselves" (122).

But I was unaware of this when I began my research. With my proposal for an autoethnographic dissertation about dissertation-writing approved, I had thought the days of the rigidly structured, tortuously written dissertations must have passed. But now, having concluded my project and moved into graduate school administration, I must say that things seem not to have changed all that much. As recently as the final months of 1998, the e-list of the Council of Graduate Schools hosted discussions that condemned the notion of collaborative dissertations and affirmed the need for the disciplining dissertation format checker. Some months after my degree was awarded, I was told by colleagues in a regional deans' meeting (who were leafing through my dissertation) that it would never have been approved at *their* institutions. This rigidity, I now believe, has to do with the liminality, and thus vulnerability to subversion, of the ritual/rhetorical space in which one becomes an academic.

In the following pages, I will first discuss some of the origins, both internal and external, of the constraints on dissertation form. I will then explore what it means to inhabit the rhetorical space of the dissertation before suggesting some of the discussions that must accompany a move toward innovation in dissertation form. In all of this, I must emphasize my belief that the dissertation, including the ritual aspects of it, serves a necessary function—we need, simply, to free the space from the arbitrary constraints that perpetuate the exclusivity of the community.

Imposition of Form

A dissertation begins, and the exertion of the conservative begins, when one accepts that words must be put to paper, that it must have a form, a progression, a tone, an audience, a title, a length, a logic—a shape. But the shape is often blurred, or perceived in caricature:

> Lynn:[3] My notion of the actual D is that it will be "original," though heavily researched, about 250 pages, several drafts depending on what my readers like or don't. Of course we want an intellectual voice in writing this thing, but I'm still trying to sort this out.

To see what dissertations should look and sound like, students often consult one of the many handbooks available. The *Guide to the Successful Thesis and*

Dissertation: A Handbook for Students and Faculty (Mauch and Birch, 1993) offers, for instance, an answer to "one of the first things a student wants to know . . . what a thesis or dissertation looks like" (225). While the modeling provided by these sources may satisfy a student's initial need, it also limits what is possible. The imposition of arbitrary rules both disciplines the writer and makes manifest the hierarchies of privilege that Code maps. It was telling that at a recent meeting for departmental graduate program liaisons at my university, a number of participants reacted with surprise when I explained that as far as the Graduate School was concerned dissertations needn't be double-spaced, nor printed on only one side of the page, and that only the binding margin was critical.

Students may also seek out dissertations to use as models only to find that the chosen volumes model traditional constraints rather than innovation. Barbara had gone to the dissertations of her advisor and recent graduates for models. Later, however, she explained:

> I don't think those were good examples of being able to really integrate the level of personal voice and experience. Not necessarily because of the topic, but I think in part because the writers were restrained by their own assumptions about what they could do.

Such self-restraint is not surprising. In another guide to dissertations, Jody Veroff explains, "stylistic rules may require you eventually to disembody yourself in your writing . . ." (1992, 159). This notion of disembodiment is disquietingly consistent with descriptions of male adolescent initiation rituals examined by van Gennep where the initiate experiences a symbolic death of the body and is then "reincorporated" into the body of the institution.

The dissertation itself is not the first hurdle, however, as a proposal generally generates boundaries for the dissertation that follows. If it's common to think, "Of course, everyone knows what a dissertation looks like," there is an equally strong sense, especially in fields and departments where students don't routinely write research proposals, that *no one* knows what a proposal looks like. What is expected may vary from one advisor to another. It may be the first three chapters of the dissertation or six pages of informal discussion. It may need to be defended or it may simply need to be approved by the advisor and possibly the committee. One can go to any university library and read dissertations; even one or two sample proposals may be hard to come by. While it is true that rigid guidelines can deter innovation, it is also true that the complete lack of guidelines can be similarly constraining.

More troubling, perhaps, the proposal seems to be the stage where potential committee members play out their own struggles of hierarchy and power. A woman in counseling psychology, for instance, explained that after months of struggling to get a proposal written, she reconstituted her committee—a move that might have been foreseen in an earlier story she had told about how her chair and one of her committee members disagreed fundamentally over the dissertation's purpose. Another woman, frustrated that members of her interdisciplinary committee could not settle on the boundaries of the project after a dozen proposal drafts, simply began data analysis. And though it seems to contradict the stories of methodological loggerheads and endless demands from committee members, it is also common for students to say of the proposal, as Lisa did, "I'm pretty much doing this on my own." At the point where the dissertation itself is being planned out, students find themselves working in an unfamiliar genre and in a politically volatile arena. Very little about the process encourages students to incorporate experiment into the plan for the dissertation.

In these women's stories, the proposal loomed as a much larger hurdle than I had imagined—a place wherein initiates are brought to a state of abjection. One woman, who early in the process was confident and enthusiastic, developed a severe writing block while working on her proposal. For a number of months, she reported some progress, then quit corresponding. A brief note indicated she was going to get it done "ASAP," but she later told of falling into depression, then of seeking treatment. She was, when I last spoke with her, trying to get three pages written for her advisor (who had been "quite supportive" the whole time). The woman who finally shifted to data analysis had gotten to the point where sitting down to write brought her to tears, and she was convinced, she said, that what she did manage to write was "awful."

Others experienced similar, if less debilitating, failures of confidence about their ability to write as an academic. Samantha's experience demonstrates the typical reaction to lack of feedback. The day she sent a partial draft of her prospectus to her chair, she wrote to me:

> I'm quite sure that I write in my own voice. I have very little confidence about speaking out in a graduate seminar. . . . However, when I write, I think/feel my voice is authoritative and I suffer less anxiety about expressing my views.

Following a lengthy period of no response to her draft, she said, "I think my advisor may be waiting for the finished product before he spends time (wastes time?) writing back." After she received the draft back with requests for revisions, including two difficult ones, she described her voice as "nonexistent." When I asked what she meant, she explained:

> The "nonexistent voice" in my revising may be due to feeling that I don't know enough, haven't read enough *and* kept careful notes—maybe because I'm supposed to be academic, informed, intelligent, somewhat of an expert and feel (know) that I'm none of those things.

She did, however, complete the revisions within the time her advisor had asked:

> [For a time] I found myself thinking about the readers' comments, suggestions, etc. and trying to defend what I had done against those remarks. When

> I sat down to work on it, it was much easier than I had imagined. Of course, I did *not* restructure or redesign my project. But I did reword and reorganize several sections and I more explicitly (sort of Dick and Jane writing) explain why I want [to approach the topic the way I do] . . . I feel hopeful about what I've done, but not confident.

Samantha had, in alluding to "Dick and Jane," exemplified the ritually necessary stripping away of old language and subsequent relearning of the language of the initiate.

Even when alternatives are imagined and survive in the prospectus, they may be stifled late in the process. Stories I'm told suggest that the tolerated level of risk-taking diminishes as the defense approaches. One writer was told to eliminate from a completed draft lengthy sections where she discussed her developing friendships with participants in her study; "So much," she said, "for my own voice." Another had spoken of her project as "pretty innovative," but last-minute revisions demanded of her had this effect:

> I was defending a dissertation that I didn't believe in, had not envisioned, and didn't like very much at all. I wondered why the hell I had been given just enough free rein to be frustrated in ways I had never imagined.

Disturbed by their own experiences and the stories they hear others tell, students often ask, "How can we do it differently when we become academics?" Those who finish, however, are acutely aware that, however unpleasant it might have been, their advisors did manage to get them through. Coupled with this is their own responsibility as academics to accomplish the same, that is, to help their students complete the process. As one recent PhD explained:

> One of the reasons I entered the e-list discussion was to warn grad students that they need to be careful about pushing too hard on those boundaries. I often see relatively established scholars loudly claiming that print is dead, that we should write hypertexts instead of static, linear texts. All I can say is, That's all well and good if you have tenure. . . . I have students work in hypertext now; although I still wouldn't suggest any of them write a diss completely in hypertext.

Hypertext thus seems to fall outside of the boundaries of what can be taken seriously within the dissertation's rhetorical space. And perhaps more than anything else, the need to be taken seriously structures the work of academics. Stacy explained why she wasn't concerned with innovative discourse:

> I'm not opposed to doing it [the dissertation] in the cookbook fashion if it means that a dissertation about the sex industry is going to get accepted, and it's going to appear in my university's graduation bulletin. There's also pressure to make a dissertation on the sex industry more academic and more scholarly because it is a stigmatized subject.

Dissertation writers who choose to explore stigmatized issues or politically sensitive topics are placed in the position of having to choose their battles. Allison explained:

> I had to justify every dot and dash. When I say that they made me justify every claim, this is consistent with a logical, analytic mode of discourse. But beneath their demands on me was more than a desire to make my dissertation the best it could be in the field. They also didn't believe that my subject's non-analytic style of discourse could be considered "real" philosophy.
>
> I edited the work and changed whatever my director wanted without much complaint because . . . I knew I could make the work be what I wanted it to after I got through the program . . . so I wrote like I knew they wanted. . . . Interestingly enough, however, this mode of expression is easy for me to slip in and out of. [My] concern was also that I was educating an entire major university philosophy department about ideas that I believe are very important . . . and I was adjusting my "voice" to one they could hear.

If we are to be heard, we must approximate the legitimated forms of expression. A parade of students carrying placards is not likely to be taken as a dissertation defense. But less extreme cases are more difficult. Can one call a textbook a dissertation? a compilation of others' works if it includes extensive annotation? a collaborative project? a hypertextual collection of original and quoted poetry? At the extreme, there is the question of whether a nonstandard dissertation *is* a dissertation. If it is not, the ritual has failed to perform its function—that is, the boundary between those to whom the ritual does pertain and those to whom it does not will have been blurred—and the possibility looms of an impostor being endowed with the *skeptron* (Bourdieu 1991, 109).

Interstice Inhabited

Much of the power of ritual, and the determining factor in whether we are taken seriously, is in the proper utterance of prescribed language. The dissertation serves this function: It involves a lengthy, intense period of writing in a discipline-specific discourse, developing fluency with a vocabulary that is often unintelligible to anyone outside the discipline. Academics often say they learned to write while writing their dissertations. All too often, this involves substituting an advisor's words for one's own. One woman, who had gotten suggestions for revision that she didn't particularly agree with, told me she made minimal changes, "just enough to get by." Another told of getting back a draft with extensive interlinear revisions that she was expected simply to adopt. Yet another explained that after struggling with her text, she appreciated her advisor's suggestions and opted to use his version "because he said it so much better than I could." Near the end, another explained, she made suggested revisions to wording that she might have resisted earlier.

Perhaps some of us can, as one participant explained it, "easily slip into and out of an academic voice." Like a mask, it can be put on and taken off. And it is difficult to dispute arguments such as Shirley Lim's, in an AAUW symposium, that women need to "learn and follow established academic forms such as dense citations. Your credibility depends on them, though they're loaded with hierarchical assumptions . . ." (Cook 1997, 23). My concern is that the habits of mind we take on in dissertation-writing determine our notions of what forms of expression are legitimate, of who should be taken seriously as competent members of the community. What is conserved by traditional dissertations—even the best of them—are the particular habits of mind that shape a vigorously dominant-culture university community. Gillian Howie and Ashley Tauchert put it strongly:

> What may start out as the price of admission, adopting alien behaviors to survive a male-run system of rewards and punishments, becomes our chosen way of operating. By a process of "interior colonization," we regulate our own behavior according to male norms. (1999, 1)

Sometimes, however, innovation in academic discourse is not seen as an issue at all: Jane, for instance, asked, "Is learning the discourse really so different than all the other compromises of spirit we make to survive/thrive/fit?" *Survival* is perhaps a fundamental cause for restraint with regard to risk and experimentation in dissertations, for students are acutely aware of their own friends and acquaintances—sometimes partners and parents—who haven't succeeded.

Bruce Lincoln, elaborating on van Gennep's model, helps explain, perhaps, the aversion to innovation and risk as dissertators make this rite of passage from one defined position to another:

> Between any two well-defined social positions, [Gennep] argues, there lies a no-man's land, a liminal period during which one has lost a previously held status without yet having gained a new one to replace it. (1991, 99)

Dissertators inhabit this liminal space. Having not yet "reincorporated," they in some sense have no identity at all. Whether intentional or not, much of the culture of graduate education reinforces these notions: the lack of formal recognition short of the PhD (coursework certification, for instance); the infrequency with which formal withdrawal procedures are used (doctoral students simply fade away); the fact that we track placement of our graduates but not of students who do not graduate. Successfully completing a dissertation that one doesn't like stifles the writerly self, but at least this self has an identity.

Whether, then, it is satisfaction with the status quo, an unconscious acceptance of it, fear of the alternatives, or the "vehement indignation and resistance" met by "any hint of reform" (Hamilton 1993, 53), there is, among those advising and writing dissertations, a strong inclination toward replication. Still, I believe that doing a dissertation is a necessary part of joining the continuing scholarly conversation. I believe there is value in the process itself—in the extended putting into words of an idea that both finds its location in and extends the scholarly conversation. Nor is the ritual to be undervalued.

I would also argue vehemently that the dissertation all too often involves unnecessary frustration, trauma, and humiliation. One woman said she felt as if she had to be "fucked" before the examining committee would allow her to leave the room following her defense, another that she completed the ordeal feeling "bruised." Gesa Kirsch, citing a "willingness to reinterpret and reevaluate difficult writing experiences in a positive light," relays the feelings of yet another about revising her dissertation: "I thought it was really very *helpful*. It almost *destroyed me* personally. It's *devastating* to get a whole dissertation with [critical comments]. But it was *very instructive*" (Kirsch's emphasis) (1993, 67). A number of the women who responded to my initial request for dissertation stories suggested that telling these stories would provide a way for them to heal from the process. There is no space set aside in van Gennep's model for healing.

I began my dissertation project suggesting that the rigidity of the dissertation silenced those who were alienated by academic discourse—silenced in that they simply could not, or would not, accommodate to the limits of academic discourse. Yet the women I was talking with had either finished their dissertations or were still in process, though at least one has since decided not to complete the dissertation. For those who finish, the term *silence* doesn't really fit, in spite of the passionate claim made by a friend who told my feminist theory class that she had been "silenced" by the dissertation process. A number of women in my study talked instead of shifting their work's focus, of finding "my own voice" seven, eight, twelve years after the dissertation was completed. And so I think what often happens is that voices from the margins are not silenced but *stifled* by putting on a mask and performing a conversion narrative prescribed by the community. If this mask is not a good fit, that is, if one does not inhabit a location of cultural dominance, its removal involves an arduous struggle to relearn one's own writerly voice.

Resistance and Intervention

How, though, to intervene? In an essay titled "Voicing the Self: Toward a Pedagogy of Resistance in a Postmodern Age," Randy Freisinger, whose class in literary nonfiction opened new writing spaces for me during my first year as a doctoral student, offers this vision:

> The fourth and final problematic term in my title—*resistance*—provides potential hope with regard to the subject, or self, and its capacity for liberatory struggle. If we can sensitize our students, make them aware of the ideology of the entrenched and empowered class and the way in which institutions often operate to maintain the status quo, we put these students in a position to fight back. (1994, 262)

Can we imagine the dissertation as a place in which we—ourselves and not just our first-year comp students—can fight back? If we wait until after the dissertation, until we are legitimate, speaking academics, we will have taken on habits of mind that are inadequate to the task. But prior to receiving the degree we are not yet recognized as fully competent members of the community; fighting back can be dismissed as adolescent rebellion. This leaves the dissertation—a period somewhat comparable to the calendar space between the ending of the old year and the beginning of the new when the carnivalesque reigns, a period of no status, a period when the initiate is liminal, interstitial, alive with *potential* to effect change.

We are left, however, with the question: If the dissertation is a space for resistance—a space in which the exclusionary, hierarchical nature of the academic community can be changed—how is it to be accomplished? We must stop thinking of dissertations as unproblematically neutral. In a composition theory class I took several years ago, Marilyn Cooper stunned me by asserting that when we teach writing we teach a world view. To extend her assertion, when advisors "teach" dissertations, they/we (shifting pronouns becomes difficult) are teaching a world view. Dissertators are no less students learning to write than are the first-year composition students who are the implied subjects of so many of our discussions about the politics of writing and teaching. We must provide a revolutionary answer to the question that first brought many of this collection's contributors together at conferences such as CCCC: What does composition's call for diversity in academic discourse have to do with us, with our dissertations?

We can, I suggest, encourage both a diversity of academic discourse and a variety of models for the ritual itself—in a word, anomaly.[4] My dissertation (1998) included resistance to the form that seem faithful to my own speaking self: essay, poetry, painting, computer graphics, visual play, performance, collaboration, conscious resistance to arbitrary format requirements. But *my* list, since I speak from a location very close to the hegemonic center, differentiated by gender, but otherwise much like the Euro-American, middle-class holders of power, will not necessarily be sufficient for others entering academe. Others have found their own alternatives. "I seem," one woman wrote, "to be writing a dissertation without footnotes." Another participant told me she had had a hard time thinking about writing her own dissertation because she could write academic papers only by imagining she was writing a letter to a friend. I also recall coming across a dissertation with a circular table of contents. In order to leave the space open to other innovation, we must encourage and tolerate the imagining of anomalies. What if a dissertation is letter, collage, autobiography, or patchwork quilt; if performance and installation from the fine arts permeate linguistic text; if the narrative of research logs infiltrates the language of scientific discourse; if whimsical illustrations intrude between even rows of text; or scientific articles appear as appendices to a science-fiction novel; if one could argue a thesis by "talking story" as one of my participants suggested, or . . .

A diversity of academic discourses is one possibility; another is to reshape the ritual. As it is currently mapped, the rhetorical space of the dissertation is congruent with the space of male initiation rituals. Yet my own experience was so unlike van Gennep's initiations that my dissertation more than flaunted discourse conventions: My committee met together over breakfast or lunch to discuss drafts; among the official members of my committee was a graduate student peer reader; my advisor suggested that I not call the public moment a defense—and so it was a "presentation." In his analysis of van Gennep's model, which emphasizes separation, transition, and incorporation, Bruce Lincoln (1991) suggests an alternative, more typically women's, idea of ritual with a pattern of enclosure, metamorphosis, and emergence. Here, the initiate does not leave the community but is taken deep into it (as many of the women in my study were drawn into personal issues by their dissertations). Neither does the initiate go through a transitional liminality but something more akin to metamorphosis. Again, the women in my study spoke of the dissertation as "transforming." Emergence following metamorphosis is not most noticeably to a higher status but into acceptance of a new level of responsibility (100–101). In what was perhaps the most positive story shared among participants in my study, Barbara explained her experience in a way that reverberates with Lincoln's alternative:

> I had a very supportive committee who looked at my draft and said to me, "Where are you in this? There's no way you should write this dissertation without us being able to see who you are and what happened to you in this, and to be able to leave a trail for other people doing research on this topic to follow." . . . In retrospect, that affirmation for myself, that both the researcher/observer/analytical voice and this very personal, sometimes very emotional, voice and experience could both be there and were legitimate, that was a new integration of myself. . . . I really had to learn how to honor a voice that I wanted to keep out completely because I didn't think it was academic enough. . . .

The necessary project, for which each of us bears responsibility, is to remap the space in which academic identities are constructed, encouraging a multitude of voices. Several issues, though, must be addressed:

- Evaluating dissertations that do not fit the standard form is more time consuming and difficult; committees must be prepared for more work and for some measure of uncertainty.
- Students and faculty need to engage in discussions about what constitutes acceptable risk—and what constitutes a dissertation.

- To provide generative models, departments should compile a bibliography of works that demonstrate—both visually and stylistically—a range of locally acceptable variations.
- Formatting rules are generally enforced by graduate school offices; these rules must be successfully challenged, which will require enlisting the support of our chairs and deans.

I will end with a challenge given me by my advisor while she and I were still talking through my dissertation's beginnings. She asked me to think about

> . . . what it would mean to *not* succeed at what you're attempting to do. . . . It seems to me it is much more than just failing to alter the dissertation repetition. But what?

End Notes

1. Vincent Tinto (1993) used this model to explain persistence and attrition among undergraduates and suggests it also may be useful for graduate students. For a discussion of the model's maleness, see Bruce Lincoln (1991), 99–102.

2. Though I did not limit my request for dissertation stories to women, those who stayed with the study were women.

3. The names of all participants in my dissertation study have been changed.

4. See Lincoln's (1989) discussion of the anomaly and its threat to normative taxonomic structures, especially pages 165–166.

Chapter Two

Behind the Accordion-Shaped Door, or Living the Questions of a Personal Academic Dissertation

Alys Culhane

The Dissertation Defense

I feel the smooth, raw, red and purple cramping,
then gasp for fresh air, an element
that is no place to be found
in this room where old ideas circle around
and where new ideas slip away under an accordion-shaped door. . . .
I listen, as the words *authority, narrative,* and *association*
are clapped together like chalky erasers
then choke on the thick, white smell of academe.
I want to put theory to practice and go beyond
the abstract. I want to talk about how for months
I'd been marking the days off my calendar,
hoping that the word period would remain
an intellectual abstraction, or at best,
a way of bringing the ramblings of freewriters to a close.
But I have no authority to tell the narrative
which is one of association:
Like the story about the time that Pete and I were in Tijuana
and I took the birth control pills in the reverse order
and how we had to hurry back to San Diego so I could see a doctor,
then after, finding out that I wasn't pregnant,
we headed north because as I said to Pete,
I can't return to that place with the three-legged dogs
and the garbage careening every which way.
As my story goes, I then knew that I loved Pete
because I understood that while he, a linear thinker
could live in nonlinear places, he did not expect the same of me.

No, I have nothing to say but like them
I say it anyways. Dazed by the relationship between language and pain
I provide the correct answers.
They let me go and I make a beeline for the nearest bathroom.
They think I'm a new person, like them.
I think, I'm the same old me.

Fiction: At the time of my dissertation defense, I wasn't having my period. However, my outside reader was having hers.

Fact: When I entered the room with the accordion-shaped door, I was unsure of how my defense was going to go because I'd written my dissertation at a distance.

Fiction: During my defense, my committee members and I talked at length about the use of narrative as a rhetorical device.

Fact: Our discussion about my use of narrative was brief and somewhat nonsensical. Two of the three male committee members contended that academic writers in training should avoid what they called "storytelling" because it's overly simplistic, subjective, touchy-feely.

Fiction: At the conclusion of my defense, I made a beeline for the women's room.

Fact: I often have bad dreams in which I'm unable to escape from the room with the accordion-shaped door.[1]

I wrote this poem shortly after I defended my dissertation, which was a defense of what I call personal-pedagogical essays—essays that in form are both personal and academic, and that in content focus on teaching. What I liked about the completed poem was that by combining elements of fact and fiction, I'd gotten at the legitimacy of first-person narrative when responding to academic issues and scenes. But about a year ago, as I sorted through old files, the crabbed scrawl of an early draft of the poem caught my attention. I then realized that the poem told only part of the story. My defense was the culmination of a two-year struggle between my belief that I should be allowed to push the stylistic boundaries of the dissertation and my committee members' concern that I not venture beyond predetermined parameters. Looking at that poem's early draft and thinking of the audience for *The Dissertation and the Discipline*—an audience of academics who also question boundaries—I sensed that a fuller account of this struggle would lend support to the claims that other contributors to this collection are making: that the entire academic community will benefit if committee members join dissertators in broadening their definition of *scholarly discourse*. I also want to expand on what I see as one of my poem's implicit claims: that advisors and committee members work most responsibly with their dissertators and avoid creating unnecessary angst and confusion when they join in living, not dismissing, the questions that such projects raise for writers and for the profession.

Rather than choose between what G. Douglas Atkins[2] (1992) calls the "academic essay" and the "personal essay," I've decided to write this chapter as a "critical essay," combining argument and personal narrative. This isn't an arbitrary decision or a retreat from academic conversation. As I discovered when writing my dissertation, the more autobiographical, emotive, and accessible form we associate with the "personal essay" actually lends itself to intra- and interdisciplinary conversation—to promoting conversation across boundaries among teachers. What immediately came to mind when I first began drafting this essay was the image of the accordion-shaped door. It was behind this door, in a brightly lit room with a view of the city skyline, that my initiation into academe both began and (nearly) ended.

I first entered this room in January 1991. Taking a seat at a long wooden table, I listened as the Midwestern University (MU)[3] composition director told me about program requirements. I left this room in March 1996 after I'd successfully completed my dissertation defense. In the five years between, I spent a great deal of time inside the room with the accordian-shaped door. There were seminars, an academic review, a preliminary exam defense. There were also innumerable meetings, the most memorable being one in which the composition graduate students took the faculty to task for "being fuzzy about procedural matters."

In time, I equated being in this room with being an academic. And so it seemed sadly ironic that it was within sight of the accordion-shaped door that my career as a teacher-writer skidded to an unexpected halt. It was early June 1995. Having completed two chapters of my dissertation and set up a meeting to receive feedback from my committee, I'd now trekked up to the fourth floor of English Hall to learn what time my current dissertation chair (D.C. for short), Committee Member #1, newly added Committee Member #2, and I would meet.[4]

As I sauntered down the hall, I heard D.C.'s voice.

"She has an MFA in creative nonfiction," she declared.

I came to a standstill. Creative nonfiction, I thought. This is my area of expertise. I wonder who else here is working in this genre? It's sure odd that no one has told me about this.

Hearing the voice of Committee Member #1, I put my good ear to the closed door.

"She did well in my essay course. She had no trouble with the contemporary material. However, I too am troubled by her atheoretical stance."

A third, more insistent voice, that of Committee Member #2, intervened.

"Yes, I'm well aware of her background and her accomplishments, but . . ."

"And she's an excellent cartoonist," added D.C.

Creative nonfiction . . . atheoretical stance . . . excellent cartoonist.

"Wait a minute," I stammered. "They're talking about me!"

No, they wouldn't be conferring like this if they'd liked my first two chapters. In the first chapter I'd provided an encapsulated history of the Romantic movement. In the second I'd shown how the contemporary expressivists had drawn upon the Romantics in forming their claims. I wasn't sure where I was going with this and the writing—third-person exposition—hadn't come easily, but that's why I'd scheduled the next day's meeting.

Standing with my head down, I let tears fall onto my running shoes. In particular, D.C. and Committee Member #1 sounded concerned, and with Committee Member #2, they concluded that what I'd written was nonsensical. When I heard them rise, I did an about-face, then ran, sobbing, in the direction of the elevator.

In preparation for the next day's meeting I reconstructed their arguments and constructed counterarguments, beginning with Committee Member #2's assertion that I had no familiarity with postmodern theory. To this I could counter that this area of study wasn't relevant to my project. Though my course readings had included smatterings of Bakhtin, Barthes, Derrida, and Foucault, I hadn't cited these individuals in my first two chapters because their ideas did not seem applicable to my focus on how the Romantics had set a precedent for expressivist thought.

I agreed with Committee Member #1's assertion that I was all over the map. However, this was at least in part due to disciplinary factionalization. At MU one's preliminary exam and proposal needed the approval of the Graduate Policy Committee (GPC), a group composed of two graduate students and a faculty member from each of the four plans: (A) Modern Studies, (B) Literary Studies, (C) Composition Studies, and (D) Creative Writing. For those in plans C and D, getting a proposal by the GPC was a major administrative accomplishment. In particular, composition and rhetoric students faced the problem of faculty in the other camps who contended that a focus on pedagogical concerns "didn't involve real research." The modern studies and literary studies folk also believed that the language of those in composition and creative writing was "too simplistic." As for the creative writing faculty, they claimed to be stymied by the other plans' discourse conventions. One GPC committee member/creative writer told me, "The overinflated language that you academics are using is a real turnoff."

In my first dissertation proposal (submitted to the GPC in December 1993) I wanted to follow up on a central assertion of the expressivists, that for students to become adept writers, teachers need to model writerly behavior. I proposed an ethnographic dissertation in which my primary source material would be two composition classes I was teaching. I'd share my writing with one group and forgo sharing it with the other. As Committee Member #1 correctly noted, this would never get by the GPC.

"What you are proposing," he said, "sounds too autobiographical. They won't pass it."

In my second proposal (which I submitted to the GPC in February 1994) I proposed a history of the expressivist movement, beginning with the Romantics and concluding with its supposed demise in the mid-1980s. However, as

Committee Member #1 again correctly noted, the GPC would nix this one because there was no discernable argument.

In my third proposal (which I submitted to the GPC in May 1994) I again proposed a history of expressivism, beginning with the Romantics and concluding with expressivism's supposed demise in the mid-1980s. However, this time, I would argue that, contrary to the assertions of many (including James Berlin and Jeanette Harris), the Romantics weren't lone thinkers; rather, in collaborating with one another, they were indirectly demonstrating that knowledge is socially constructed. The same, I contended, holds true of the contemporary expressivists, who are strong advocates of collaborative practices.[5]

I was pleased to learn that the GPC had passed this proposal, though, as a student member told me, it didn't pass on the strength of my argument. Rather, they passed it on the advice of Committee Member #1, who, after some pleading on my part, attended the meeting.

"Your proposal was confusing to us," the student member said. "We needed assurance that you were capable of writing a dissertation on your proposed subject."

Now it seemed like my committee members were seeking such assurance. As I continued to sort through their objections to my first two chapter drafts, I also examined D.C.'s claim that, because she'd worked closely with me, she couldn't understand why my chapters lacked focus. Shortly before I began working on the first draft of my dissertation proposal, the recently tenured faculty member informed me that she'd be spending the following year overseas. When she returned and read my first chapter, she reminded me again of what I'd been told at my preliminary exam defense—that the purpose of a dissertation is to demonstrate that the candidate can formulate a thesis, then support this thesis with the claims of established theorists.

"I've been trying to do this," I sputtered. "And quite obviously, I've failed. What I'd like to do," I added, "is return to my original idea and write about writing alongside my students."

D.C. leaned back in her chair, then crossed her arms.

"Could we get together in a few weeks?" I queried. "I'd like to have three chapters done by November because that's when I want to start applying for jobs."

D.C. opened her planner and quickly flipped through the pages. Previous to her overseas trip, we'd met once every two weeks.

"How about we meet on October thirty-first 1 P.M.?"

"If you have any cancellations, please let me know," I replied, adding, "I'd like to defend in the spring because the department doesn't offer fifth-year teaching assistantships."

"You'll finish by spring," she said, closing her planner.

Later I'd speculate about why our subsequent meetings were so rushed. Maybe D.C was uneasy because this was her first go-round as a dissertation chair. Or maybe she was tired of hand-holding.

D.C's response to my plans confused me because it went against her central assertion that composition and rhetoric welcome the insights of those scholars who push the boundaries of academic writing and encourage their students to do the same. In her course "Narratives and Theories of Literacy," she had applauded Peter Elbow's (1991) refutation of David Bartholomae's (1985) claim that it's the job of compositionists to train students to fit into the conventions of academic discourse. She was also the most accepting of my narratively based seminar papers, all of which in one way or another championed the Elbowian perspective.

In March 1994 I handed D.C. two extensively revised chapters. In May, after receiving what I felt was minimal feedback, I suggested that we meet with my other committee members so that I might find out whether I was on the right track.

On re-entering the room with the accordion-shaped door, I felt confident, believing that once my committee knew the big picture, they'd be more willing to provide me with advice. I also believed that, because the GPC proposal dictates were behind us, they'd be more accepting of my doing a nontraditional dissertation that used narrative to make and explore arguments.

After taking our seats we talked about the weather and the doings of the local baseball team. A long, uncomfortable silence followed. A wave of nervousness passed over me. Then it began.

I momentarily gave in, agreeing that while I'd given dissertation-writing a fair shot, academic writing wasn't my forte. I offered no resistance to the committee's collective assertion that because I was a good teacher, I should find work in a community college. Yes, I thought, what all three are saying makes sense. If I landed a job at a research institution (and this was a big if) where creative and scholarly writing are thought to be oxymoronic terms, I wouldn't get tenure. Therefore, it wasn't imperative that I produce a dissertation. Or was it? Much to my surprise, the person who spoke next was the me who wasn't a quitter.

"Well," I said brightly, "I want to finish. Maybe we could set up a strict schedule. I'll turn in drafts to D.C. Then she can pass them on to the two of you."

After yet another long silence, D.C. spoke.

"Who's going to chair your committee?"

"You are, aren't you?"

"I'm sorry, Alys, but I can't. . . ."

"And at this time, neither I nor Committee Member #2 feel comfortable about taking on the job," interjected Committee Member #1.

"Maybe you can get someone in the creative writing department to head your committee," suggested Committee Member #2.

"But," I protested, "all my coursework has been in composition and rhetoric."

"It doesn't matter. Your degree will be in English Studies," said Committee Member #2.

"Can I get an extension on my teaching assistantship?"

"I'm afraid," said Committee Member #1, "that's an impossibility. We don't offer fifth-year extensions. You could apply for a lectureship."

"But lectureships pay less than teaching assistantships."

"I'm sorry. But let us know if there's any other way we might help you out."

Fifteen minutes after the meeting began, I thanked my committee members for their help, stumbled to the door, fumbled with the latch, then staggered into the narrow hallway. I was now on the outside looking in.

My partner, Pete, suggested I move with him to Clemson, where he was working on a master's in professional communication. After we'd settled into our new digs, an 8-by-24 trailer, I considered my options. I could (1) abandon the idea of a dissertation and write a work of creative nonfiction; (2) attempt to enroll in another PhD program; or (3) resume working on my dissertation and, when nearly done, try to assemble a new committee.

I chose Option 3, but only after I'd received input from a former teacher, who, after reading my draft, said that this option was my best choice. "Quite clearly," she said in a lengthy email message, "you did an incredible amount of research. But your attempt to write in an academic voice isn't working. I suggest that you start all over, but this time, write your dissertation in your own voice. If a reconstituted committee doesn't like what you produce, you can turn your dissertation into a book, then next year, pitch it to publishers." I had mixed feelings about her response, for I didn't relish the thought of beginning anew. But I was also elated because it again looked like the acquisition of a PhD was within my grasp.

The answer to the question What should I write about? came to me a week later as I set up a work area at the far end of the trailer. I was pinning up a yellowed *New Yorker* cartoon, one in which a man, sitting at a typewriter, is staring out into space, as are the innumerable mongrels that surround him. Standing behind him is a woman who says, "Write about dogs."

Yes, I thought, I've been missing the obvious. My areas of expertise are the history of the essay and expressivist pedagogy. I could expand on an earlier seminar paper in which I defined the personal-pedagogical essay. I could draw further on my expertise and interests. My feet propped up on a box of Arm & Hammer laundry soap, I began essaying, working inductively and letting the content dictate the form. To my great joy, the writing came somewhat easier than it had previously, in part because I was in form and content relying on the insights of other compositionist/essayists, some of whom included Lynn Z. Bloom, Ken Macrorie, Donald Murray, Donald McQuade, and Nancy Sommers.

I'd also distanced myself from the voices of my committee members, whose dictates were to write in an academic voice, defer to sources, and be up front with my argument. Yet I say the writing came *somewhat* easier because I didn't have an immediate audience. I was also unsure as to what the outcome of my endeavors would be.

In late October 1995, two months after I'd left town, the accordion-shaped door opened a crack. One day as I was writing, the phone rang. I fingered the phone cord and listened to the far-off voice of Committee Member #2. Then I hung up and ran into the kitchen.

"Pete," I said, "you won't believe what just happened."

"What?"

"That was Committee Member #2. He said that a member of the creative writing department is interested in chairing my dissertation committee."

"Committee Member #2 said this?"

"Yes."

"Do you believe it?"

"No."

"Must be some kind of joke, doncha think?"

"Has to be."

"Well, he isn't completely on your side," remarked Pete.

"How's that?"

"While he appears to have your interests at heart, he's saying you're a creative writer, not a compositionist."

I felt conflicted. I was relieved to be one step closer to graduating. However, I also knew that my five-year stint in a factionalized program had adversely affected my thinking. I'd become a compartmentalist, seeing myself as a member of plan C, composition and rhetoric—someone who, when she wrote, was talking to and citing the authorities in her field. I hadn't entered MU's program with this mind-set. Rather, this was the end result of being in a graduate student in a department that was divided into separate subdisciplines. Consequently, I, a compositionist, didn't want to write a creative dissertation. Yet I also didn't want to be labeled a compartmentalist.

When I spoke to my former teacher, she recommended that I deal head-on with this business of disciplinary factionalization by asserting that the personal-pedagogical essay uses first-person narration and accessible language to reach a broad-based readership. This complemented my belief that such works can promote much-needed interdisciplinary conversation. I resumed writing, although now I pictured the creative writer (whom I'd never met) as a member of my larger audience.

When I had what I thought was a reader-based prose draft in hand, I phoned him.

"Sure, I'm open to graduate students writing nontraditional dissertations," he said. "If we want larger audiences for our work, we need to be pushing the boundaries of the academic dissertation. What are you proposing to do?"

In a halting voice, I told him that I was fairly far along in the process of writing a dissertation on the subject of personal-pedagogical essays.

"Like the work of Richard Hugo and William Stafford?"

"Yes," I replied.

"What you're doing sounds interesting," he said. "I'll sign on as your dissertation chair. Send me a draft of your work and I'll reply with a written response."

Chair #2 turned out to be a very open and fair-minded individual—in fact, more so than I'd originally given him credit for being. I couldn't, at this point, ask for anything more, except perhaps, a committee who thought as he did.

Our talk also helped me overcome a major stumbling block—the prohibition against using first person in the dissertation. This obstacle fell away when Chair #2 okayed my including a metanarrative on my research process plus a final autobiographical chapter in which I speculated about the pros and cons of writing alongside my students.

After getting Chair #2's first set of comments, I began the task of putting together a second committee. Because I did so from South Carolina, this was a time-consuming process. MU required dissertation candidates to have five-member committees. I figured that at least three of the five members of the composition faculty would refuse, and I was reluctant to ask professors in the other plans because I hadn't taken any courses with them.

After Chair #2 approached them, D.C. and Committee Member #2 agreed to be on my committee. Committee Member #1 also suggested that I send him a draft. Three weeks before my defense, however, he sent an email saying that he'd forgo attending, because he thought I needed to be more up front with my central argument. Having no one else to ask, I coerced the current English department chair into taking Committee Member #1's spot. The fifth vacancy was filled by my former teacher plus a part-time professor whose area was creative nonfiction. (According to the MU dictates, an outside reader and a part-timer together equal one committee member.)

My defense was held in March 1996. After trooping into the room with the accordion-shaped door, we sat in a circle, D.C. and Committee Member #2 taking seats near the door. That the two had agreed to attend was as much of a surprise to me as was Committee Member #2's willingness to find me a new dissertation chair. Their appearance, I hoped, was verification of my dissertation's success.

After talking some about the weather, they began questioning in earnest. Why, the committee members asked, had I insisted on writing a nontraditional dissertation? What prompted me to write about personal-pedagogical essays? Why did I think that the personal essay was more accessible than the academic article? What was my rationale in including a detailed description of my research process in my dissertation? Of what benefit is it to readers to have nonfiction writers push the boundaries of fact and fiction? And what are the pros and cons of narrative structure in academic writing? When the committee had finished with its friendly interrogation, my new chair politely asked me to step out into the hallway. As I wiped my sweaty hands on my skirt, I presumed I hadn't passed, in part because I thought the questions had been too easy. I assured myself that this being composition studies, dissertation defenses were more egalitarian. Or the questions were simplistic because the committee already agreed that in being tenacious, I'd earned what a former MU English department chair had once called "the highest degree in the land."

It was as Committee Member #2 asked me back into the room that the real reason for the supposedly overgeneral questions came to mind. In *Letters to a Young Poet* Rainer Rilke (1972) tells his young protégé, "Live the questions." As I took my seat, I realized that this was what I'd done. I'd created a dissertation that was precisely what my original committee had eschewed—an extended personal-pedagogical essay. Though the writing had had its painful moments, I suspected this document would serve me in good stead. As a writer, I would continue to work in this form, and as a teacher, I would encourage my students to do the same.

A Postscript

Since that cold March day, I've continued, as both a writer and teacher, to push the boundaries of academic writing. In my dissertation I argued for the inclusion of narrative in academic conversations. But as I've recently been thinking, why not encourage academic writers, including dissertators, to work in multiple genres? And why not let them experiment with fictive devices such as composite characters and invented dialogue? And why not allow for the use of multiple voices? Here, then, are more questions for future dissertators and committee members to take up and live out, not simply dismiss.

Endnotes

1. In the five years I've been working on this chapter, I've heard of many changes in the MU program, including the removal of the accordian-shaped door. While my essay may now appear dated, I think it demonstrates that the personal-academic writing debate isn't an abstraction but an issue that many academics, theoretically and practically, at MU and beyond, still grapple with.

2. In *Estranging the Familiar,* G. Douglas Atkins (1992) distinguishes between the "academic article" and the "personal essay." As Atkins defines it, the academic article is objective, conclusive, close-ended, expositionally driven, hierarchical, and nonemotive. Conversely, the personal essay is subjective, exploratory, open-ended, narratively driven, egalitarian, emotive, and speculative. According to Atkins, the critical essay has characteristics of both.

3. MU, writes Robert Pirsig, author of *Zen and the Art of Motorcycle Maintenance* (1975), means neither yes nor no. It's also not coincidental that the setting of Jim Hynes' book *The Lecturer's Tale* (2001) is also Midwestern University, for his work, like mine, considers the problems that go hand-in-hand with disciplinary factionalization.

4. When I first drafted this essay, I gave myself permission to name names out of a shared belief with surgeon/writer Sherwin B. Nuland (2001) who argues,

> Writing makes it possible to find out what we think, often for the first time. It is a process that will be totally honest if we are willing to feel those emotions which are coming forth from preserved memory and to put them down on paper uncensored. While this process is taking place, there can be no consideration of ethics, confidentiality, or even loyalty to participants. There is only the reality of what the writer feels to be the truth of what he is describing. (129)

I later opted to use pseudonyms, in the hope that my readers would focus on the events and issues rather than on specific characters.

5. At about the same time I was dealing with the GPC, Sherrie Gradin published *Romancing Rhetorics* (1994), an excellent study that connects Romantic, expressive, and social constructionist thought.

Chapter Three

Participation: On an Ethics of Beginnings[1]

Fred Arroyo

> *The notion of self-understanding as an ethical project calls for the universal human perception that each person or group is an other among others. That is, nobody has a monopoly on truth. . . .*
>
> *Only the cultural polyglot who studiously apprehends other local knowledges in the mutual give-and-take of engaged conversation can hope to inhabit a world broader than his or her parish of birth.*
>
> —Renato Rosaldo (1999), "A Note on Geertz as a Cultural Essayist"

In this conversation about reinventing the dissertation in composition and rhetoric, I question the pervasive belief that scholars can only start by creating narratives that are somehow *better than anyone else's*.[2] As the Native American scholar Karl Kroeber (1993) tells it, the American notion of continual progress "destroys diverse modes of imagining" (35) and, moreover, does not take into account the ethical project of self-understanding in relation to others who think and imagine differently through their local knowledge. Surely, all emerging scholars identify problems they want to address in a way that helps a discipline change how they see these problems. I, for instance, just completed a dissertation, "Discursive Inheritances and the Debt of Composition: Beginnings, Memories, and the Voice of Participation," where I argue that as composition and rhetoric (seemingly) becomes more sophisticated and professionalized, it forgets those discursive inheritances to which it is indebted. Thus composition and rhetoric aspires to master and progress beyond certain binaries—reading/writing; rhetoric/poetics; practice/theory; pedagogy/scholarship; teacher/student; classroom/culture—and yet, I suggest, these very binaries should not be forgotten. I argue that the binary between reading and writing, for example, is an inheritance we should engage as a resource of hope; this binary helps the discipline locate its intentions and methods, its *discursivity,* and it continually helps me to imagine what literacy can mean and what my literacy practices can create within the discipline. I'm extremely grateful for what my literacy practices have created—the freedom of my education, the opportunity to participate within the humanities through my reading, writing, and teaching, the fulfillment of a long dream and the beginning of a challenging future: I am now an assistant professor of rhetorical theory and cultural studies at Saint Louis University. I acknowledge the debt I owe to my discursive inheritances, and I don't want composition and rhetoric to progress in such a way that it forgets the possible power literacy and learning can have for one's life. To this end, I analyze in my dissertation three tropes or discursive sites—*beginnings, memories,* and *participation*—that help composition and rhetoric recollect important discursive inheritances.

I do want my dissertation to create change; I don't want composition and rhetoric to simply progress. I want to be a vital member of the discipline's rich tradition, yet I hope to respond critically to that tradition. My position is paradoxical. How can I criticize that which I aspire to inherit and belong to? How can I create both change and continuation? How can I critique the agonistic rhetorical tradition[3] from within that same language and tradition? If I critique the discipline, am I beginning to separate myself from it?

These questions are indebted to an authoritative, compelling philosophical history I cannot presently include. We might recall, however, Jacques Derrida's "Structure, Sign, and Play" (1978), where he tells us that, "We have no language—no syntax and no lexicon—which is foreign to this history; *we can pronounce not a single destructive proposition which has not had to slip into the form, the logic, and the implicit postulation of precisely what it seeks to contest*" (280–81, my emphasis). Derrida suggests that if I, a teacher-scholar heavily indebted to and imbricated within the discursivity of composition and rhetoric, begin to critique the power the discipline has achieved through theoretical sophistication and progress, then I also begin to question the very grounds or authority from which I make my critique, since my critique emerges from and slips back into the same language I'm criticizing. Can I propose that I am located within a special circumstance—a special language—that allows me to stand outside and apart from the circumstance criticized? Can I ever stand outside those (Western) literacy practices that are so crucial for my beginnings?

So much of my graduate education was predicated on being "critical" and creating "original interventions," my peers and I imagining hostile readers of our texts—a teacher, a mentor, or the editor of a journal who would tell us our work was not political enough, did not create radical change, and did not bring the final say to a problem. In this environment that valorized original interventions and masked our reliance on others to provide the terms for our participation, I couldn't find a way to participate. I am a Puerto Rican American with only a few peers in the discipline to turn to and was often the only person of color in a classroom, so I frequently felt that if I didn't critically intervene, who would? I found the possibility of participation even more perplexing in a cultural climate where my sympathies and aims seem unquestionable. I must desire to critically question and end current practices precisely because of the lack of Latino peers, which suggests that composition and rhetoric excludes the participation of Latinos. But, again, how can I call into question a discipline I want to participate in? How can I critically respond to, recall, and reflect upon the intentions and methods of the discipline in a way that allows me to participate fully, while inviting other Latinos and people of color to participate? There is, to my way of thinking, an implicit paradox within narratives of change and, according to Derrida, within language use: Every time I try to work outside the center the language or the discipline offers me, I still find myself within a circle—more importantly, I find myself within this circle even though composition studies has a long history of excluding the participation of someone like myself. I am always within the circle, within the center, no matter how marginalized I may seem. But does this mean that the work I do in composition and rhetoric can never be critically important?

What I want to do is explore how this paradox—that we are always within the language and history we critique, that we are always within the circle no matter how marginalized we may seem—is actually a heuristic, one that has helped me to create and locate a site of *participation,* an *ethics of beginnings.* Creating an ethics of beginnings means locating a site from which I can responsibly participate in the discipline's tradition and history without forgetting the importance of my literacy practices; it means locating a site from which I can invite others to participate in the discipline, too, without forgetting the power their literacy practices can have within the discipline. In this way, an ethics of beginnings helps me to initiate what Renato Rosaldo (1999) describes as an ethical project of self-understanding, a project conducted in relation to others whose literacy practices are different from my own. Because the paradox of participation is so inherent to Western notions of language and thought, and because composition and rhetoric helps to archive, retrieve, and disseminate such notions, I must engage (not ignore, not try to speak outside of) this archive in order to locate sites of discursivity that help me to begin my participation *and* face the difficulty. I will presently turn to one such site of discursivity, one that speaks to the difficulties of beginning within a discipline, that illustrates some of the contentious issues I struggled with in my dissertation, and that illuminates the ethics of beginnings I'm proposing.

In "Whose Voice Is It Anyway? Rodriguez's Speech in Retrospect" (1997), Victor Villanueva argues that what makes Rodriguez's memoir *(Hunger of Memory,* 1982) so affirming for U.S. English teachers is that, basically, it's an "immigrant's story," one that relieves the "anxiety" teachers have when teaching nonstandard or non-English speakers because it tells us there is no difference between the immigrant and the minority (110). Both bear the difficulty of linguistic assimilation, but in doing so they become Americans, their presence subtly changing how we think about standard English and what it means to be an American. Villanueva takes Rodriguez to task for this story, arguing that there is a difference between the immigrant's and the minority's story, the "difference between choice and colonization" (111). The immigrant chooses to come to America, desiring, most often, to become someone new. The colonized, however, are forced to become Americans, and historically this forced Americanization happened when the United States' borders and land holdings expanded: when the United States took possession of cultural homelands, forcing Native Americans onto reservations, and when African Americans were forcibly brought to America as slaves. And there is, of course, for Villanueva a greater difference between the immigrant and the minority: that of racism. Minorities will be marked as different, regardless of how well they speak or write English. For Villanueva, therefore, "language alone [is] not the secret to assimilation" (115).

Villanueva's essay, written after he attended a 1986 National Council of Teachers of English (NCTE) luncheon address by Rodriguez, is frequently paired in anthologies alongside an excerpt from Rodriguez's *Hunger of Memory*.[4] Someone has decided these pieces have value together, and yet, rhetorically, it seems they only have value when Villanueva's response is placed after Rodriguez. I imagine, to put this another way, that Rodriguez and Villanueva are brought together to begin a dialogue, though I have a feeling that Villanueva's response is presumed to be the correct, critical, progressive position, and this presumption doesn't seem right to me.

I am struck by how much of my education has become a part of both Rodriguez's and Villanueva's stories, though I often feel I learned to forget Rodriguez's story. Sometimes, as I stated earlier, others assume that I must desire to critically question and end the current practices of English studies, precisely because of a lack of Latino peers, which suggests English studies excludes underrepresented others. How could I turn to Rodriguez when his belief in assimilation has not changed the participants in higher education? What good—what changes—has his story created? In graduate school I frequently felt extreme pressure to create change. But how could I question what Rodriguez so eloquently spoke of as my possibilities within language? And how could I forget how Rodriguez's words spoke to me as if he and I are intimates, as if I shared a secret with him that he turned into a public act of community—an act that shared some of my worse fears and sources of shame:

> At last he feels that he belongs in the classroom, and this is exactly the source of the dissatisfaction he causes. To many persons around him, he appears too much the academic. There may be some things about him that recall his beginnings—his shabby clothes; his persistent poverty; or his dark skin (in those cases when it symbolizes his parents' disadvantaged condition)—but they only make clear how far he has moved from his past. He has used his education to remake himself. (65)

In order to honor Rodriguez's words (and my memory of them), I decided I needed to reflect on how and why I read the texts I do, and from these experiences I needed to begin to value what I could achieve through my literacy practices. So what I did was actually read Rodriguez again. I read his *Hunger of Memory* as a narrative of loss, as a book of mourning that never fully replaces what has died in his life. He tells us that through language he became an American citizen, but in doing so he experienced a painful loss that will never heal: As a little boy he has lost his home; as an adult he understands he can never go home (22; see also 23 and 27). Assimilation could never repair how rent his life had become, could never console his grief. Rodriguez writes:

> You who read this act of contrition should know that by writing it I seek a kind of forgiveness—not yours. The forgiveness, rather, of those many persons whose absence from higher education permitted me to be classed a minority student. I wish they would read this. I doubt they ever will. (153)

But some have. I have read his words, and I mourn those many who are still absent from higher education. Rodriguez knew, too, like Villanueva I believe, that there were much larger forces that would keep others out, and so his words ring with great ethical urgency as we teach those who begin to enter and sit down in our classes.

I am deeply moved, moreover, by the multiple meanings this "act of contrition" might have. Contrition is caused by or enacts a sincere, deep sense of remorse, and there is in Rodriguez's act of contrition a deep and painful acknowledgment that he has done something terribly wrong. Yes, many will suggest that Rodriguez regrets accepting the label *minority* and the few academic privileges he received from this label, and this is exactly one of the reasons why he argues for assimilation. But there is much more ambivalence here than many of us have been willing to hear. It seems to me Rodriguez is responding to the vicious forces that label others and squelch their possibilities. Assimilation was one answer, but he did not come willy-nilly to it. I hear, moreover, not an answer but a strategy to ethically struggle *within textuality,* a struggle between what Rodriguez wanted to speak for and how he formed those expressions in words.

Throughout *Hunger of Memory* we find Rodriguez's (subjective) struggle against structures (labels, education, and society) that would deny his very being. Rather than tokenizing his writing as an example of assimilation, we need to help our students understand how Rodriguez can help them in their understanding of and struggle with academic discourse. We often suggest that we should criticize Rodriguez for assimilating, precisely because we don't think students should assimilate, and yet we do so in a paradoxical, unethical way: Politically and on the theoretical level, students should question and criticize assimilation, and yet in writing, on the practical level, students have to assimilate by learning specific conventions that speak to academic contexts, and thus they must demonstrate that they can assimilate within and beyond first-year writing requirements. I am suggesting that composition and rhetoric has a desire to represent itself as a discipline with progressive, critical intentions, in theory that is; yet our practices appropriate Rodriguez's writing in a way that undercuts the efficacy his writing could have within our classrooms and for our students' language awareness. Rodriguez can help students to understand how they can "come to value written words as never before," how they learn from what "is most personal," while being "determined at the same time to have [their] words seen by strangers" (187–88).

In engaging with this struggle, students, too, can respond to the vicious forces that label and squelch possibilities. They, too, can struggle *within textuality;* they can struggle *within* the things they want to speak for and how they form those expressions in words. They, too, can struggle *within acts of contrition, within* the literacy practices they bring into the classroom and the literacy practices they encounter in the classroom. And then taken together, I believe there arises the possibility of students locating their *beginnings:* a stance or site of learning where what is most essential in their lives must participate in relation to others who may contest, change, and even try to suppress what is so essential. In locating their beginnings, students will have a greater understanding of the power their literacy practices can have.

What I am suggesting has further implications, however. Victor Villanueva fails to acknowledge that Rodriguez's story is essential to his own, that Rodriguez, in a very complex way that we must acknowledge, is an essential presence that helps us read Villanueva's story. Rodriguez's story should continue within Villanueva's; it should truly be a part of a larger memory and a site of retrospection and debt. Likewise, I cannot tell the story of what language can become if I repress or forget either Rodriguez's story or Villanueva's story. I must read their stories together; I must create dialogic relations. If not, only one story rules how I listen to and use language. Not only do I deny the possibility of participation, I squelch the very ethics of beginnings.

I want to extend this exploration a bit further through the work of Walter J. Ong (1977), whose sense of "audience" is central to my work, in order to open a dialogue with Villanueva's writing. Ong writes:

> The historian, the scholar or the scientist, and the simple letter writer all fictionalize their audiences, casting them in a made-up role and calling on them to play the role assigned.
>
> Because history is always a selection and interpretation of those incidents the individual historian believes will account better than other incidents for some explanation of totality, history . . . is a making . . . [The historian's] selection of events and his way of verbalizing them so that they can be dealt with as "facts," and consequently the overall pattern he reports, are all his own creation, a making. No two historians say exactly the same thing about the same given events, even though they are both telling the truth. (74)

Villanueva's work is so much about rewriting history, about telling other stories that stand as a counterpoint to the given, acknowledged, "official" history. But so much of his work is simply a fiction: His writing is a "selection and interpretation" of what he believes will give a better "account" (than Rodriguez's) of what language can do, and his writing "is [surely] a making" that "verbalizes" his beliefs and calls forth an audience who will "play the role [he has] assigned" for them. It is odd for me to imagine that audience, though. Near the end of "Whose Voice Is It Anyway?", Villanueva criticizes Rodriguez for identifying with D. H. Lawrence, a writer Villanueva feels was co-opted from his working class background (116). Villanueva then places Lawrence in opposition to W. B. Yeats—a move that further accentuates Villanueva's rewriting of history and creation of (in Ong's terms) a fiction. For instance, while acknowledging that Lawrence's "mastery of the English language cannot be gainsaid," Villanueva identifies with W. B. Yeats, "Anglo and Irish, assimilated but with a well-fed memory of his ancestry, master of the English language, its beauty, its traditions—and voice of the colony" (117). It's that phrase about Lawrence—"cannot be gainsaid"—so literate, beautiful, and rhetorically effective, that gives me pause. It shows me the power of Villanueva's writing, and it shows me how Villanueva is indebted to a history of language and culture that knows of Yeats *and* Lawrence. It also shows me the politics of a language: how Villanueva must acknowledge that Lawrence existed and that he is important (just as is Rodriguez), even though Villanueva "would rather" align himself with Yeats. In aligning himself with Yeats, Villanueva also calls on his audience—that audience he's cast, as Ong says, into a "made-up role"—to identify with Yeats too, to identify with the "voice [Villanueva's voice?] of the colony."

What I am analyzing is how Villanueva is making a fictional history where Yeats is the "good" master of the English language and Lawrence is the "bad," when the truth is that they are *both* masters of the English language. To put this another way, Yeats is an example of a writer who masters but is not mastered by the English language, while Lawrence is an example of one who masters *and* is mastered by the English language. Villanueva imagines a particular audience and tries to shape that audience's response to these two figures: He imagines a literate audience that values the power of the English language, and he creates an audience that will draw critical lines between those who (seemingly) help a political cause (the colonized like Yeats and Villanueva) and those who won't (the co-opted like Lawrence and Rodriguez).

There is, nevertheless, such an inherent paradox to Villanueva's history: He identifies with the colonized (a fiction in itself) though he is heavily indebted to and a vital participant within the structures of language and education that seemingly reify the colonial practices he is against. (All one has to do, for instance, is analyze how Villanueva's rhetoric constantly wavers between identification and division, which I briefly began in the preceding paragraph.) His distinction between the immigrant and the minority (colonized) also seems rather unclear, in fact, quite unhistorical for the multiethnic, multilingual nation I teach in. Yes, there is a difference between the minority and the immigrant. But in the day-to-day of the classroom, how does this distinction help me to face my students? Because I am a "minority," do I only identify with other minorities and negate the presence of the many immigrants in my class? And how many of the students in my basic writing classes, which I taught while working on my dissertation at the University of Wisconsin-Milwaukee, were the minority or the colonized? Most often they were the majority, and most often they didn't need a teacher to indoctrinate them in the ideological nuances of language. They understood, it seems to me, that they needed to create their own sense of language awareness, an awareness that neither fully reinscribes dominate language practices nor simply celebrates the languages of their homes and communities.

I understand and feel the ethos of Villanueva's position, nevertheless. My memory is colored by my deep awareness of my father's third-grade education and his childhood of work in the fields of Puerto Rico. I also have deep memories of work in the fields of southwestern lower Michigan and memories of the racism and the systemic forces that continue to oppress Latinos and seemingly guarantee a future of menial, deathly work. (I remember constantly those friends who committed suicide in the face of this future.) And I have memories of a larger family, of Spanish as the primary language of home and community, and I am, of course, thrown back into memories when I face the Latino, Laotian, Serbian, Hmong, African American, and Native American students who enter my classrooms. But I consider my current life a blessing. I am privileged to do what I do, to do it with love, passion, intelligence, and responsibility, especially since I never had the goals nor the intentions many current students have. How did it ever happen, in fact, that I left the world of hard physical labor to the safe labor of the mind, this beautiful life of working with words? There are many deep memories—these are all a part of them. There are memories I will never deny. Yet they won't create the only history or story I will listen to: For there are many of us—Rodriguez and Villanueva included—creating new *beginnings*. Together we are each telling stories of the power that our literacy practices and learning have in our lives, and how we want future generations to turn to these different stories, so they can begin to tell their multiple stories and histories.

I am suggesting, finally, that together Richard Rodriguez's and Victor Villanueva's literacy narratives bring special value to my literacy narrative and my intellectual history, which, in turn, helps me to begin my ethical participation within composition and rhetoric. I wouldn't be the particular literacy teacher and scholar I am had it not been for Rodriguez *and* Villanueva. I won't, therefore, draw critical or theoretical lines between them or insist on distinctions that make my narrative *better*. Rodriguez's and Villanueva's narratives create different arcs, but when I follow each arc, I suddenly find I am of the center of a vibrant, living, emerging circle, a circle of language, history, and life that does not allow me to deny the importance of my literacy practices nor my participation within the tradition of composition and rhetoric. Together, Rodriguez and Villanueva help me create the ethics of my beginnings: My dissertation must responsibly recognize and verify how and why I found it possible to participate within the discipline's tradition and history, without forgetting the importance of *both* Rodriguez and Villanueva within my participation; and my dissertation must also contribute to what composition and rhetoric can become and how it allows others to have the chance to shape their lives through the opportunities their literacy practices create.

Surely, all scholars need to examine their participation within composition and rhetoric. But what I have tried to expose through my particular engagement with Rodriguez and Villanueva is the question of how much I want to participate within the discipline. How much do I want to participate? What will I do to define my participation through my dissertation? How responsible will I be in creating the relations of this participation?[5]

The dissertation is a discursive site that locates an emerging scholar's intention of participation, and to even consider responsible participation is to begin within the discipline without foreclosing the possibility of relations. A dissertation, therefore, is a beginning dialogue between the graduate student one has been and the professional one is becoming, and it is a dialogue that speaks for the scholarly work an emerging scholar aspires to contribute to the discipline. A dissertation is not just a requirement, in other words, nor is it the *singular* document of *a* professional[ized] master of a subject. Instead, the dissertation creates *beginnings:* Graduate students enter into the real, unconcluded process of responsibility for themselves and the relations they are creating within the ongoing conversation that structures the discipline. To this end, a dissertation of participation *speaks* a conversation of beginnings: It is a highly textualized composition that echoes the many conversations one is beginning (in my case conversations with Rosaldo, Rodriguez, Villanueva, my memories and the future I aspire to live); the dissertation speaks—in its textuality, in its composition—about what belief means in recalling and responding to the discipline's intentions and methods.[6]

I can never start—begin—from zero. If I deny my debt to others and deny their presence in the discipline with me, willing myself forward by the light of originality, I thwart and destroy the very possibility of beginnings. If instead my dissertation requires me to recall and respond to the intentions and methods of the discipline, what I accept as my discursive inheritances, I must also remember the necessary role my literacy practices have in my life, the affirming, nurturing experiences at the center of reading and writing—even if the politics of literacy seem to suggest that I can be co-opted by the very (Western) "literacy" I participate within. My literacy practices are a discursive inheritance I will never deny—I exist within the circle of my literacy.

Some will object that I am being conservative, traditional, and nostalgic (*we need to create change, not regress*). So be it. I do not understand tradition as that which I must work against and distance myself from. The memory of a tradition is not simply a museum or an archive deposited with continuous, familiar ideals, nor is tradition a structure that will provide me with foundational rules needed to preserve my self-certainty and that of a discipline. Instead, I think of tradition and memory as open-ended encounters of otherness that remove me from my self-certainty, that help me to revise my ways of seeing and doing, and that also will help us to reinvent what composition and rhetorical studies can become *and* who it can include.[7]

End Notes

1. I wish to acknowledge the influence Renato Rosaldo's *Culture and Truth* (1989) has had in my writing this essay, particularly his discussion of structure, subjectivity, and agency.

2. See Sherrie Gradin's (2000) "Revitalizing Romantics, Pragmatics, and Possibilities for Teaching."

3. See Ong, especially pages 216–17 in *Interfaces of the Word* (1977), as well as his *Fighting for Life: Contest, Sexuality, and Consciousness* (1981).

4. See Villanueva, *Living Languages: Contexts for Reading and Writing* (1997).

5. See Gadamer's dialectical definition of *participation* and *tradition* in his "The Hermeneutics of Suspicion" (1984, 64).

6. Edward W. Said's "An Ethics of Language" (1974) and his *Beginnings: Intention and Method* (1985) have influenced my thoughts on *beginnings*.

7. See Gerald Bruns' "What is Tradition?" (1991).

Chapter Four

Other Than Oedipus
Sideshadowing Tales of Dissertation Authority

Nancy Welch

The Female Oedipus

Early in my graduate career I read an essay by a feminist psychoanalytic theorist, Toril Moi (1989), that located the drive for knowledge pre-Oedipally, prior to an understanding of institutional prohibitions and social taboos. The pre-Oedipal stage, Moi argued, is not a time of undifferentiated oneness—what Freud called primary narcissism—but of keen self- and other-awareness. The infant feels with wonder and terror the fragmentation of its body and strives to create an always-changing coherence. In Moi's story of wonder, terror, and desire to integrate, I believed I'd found an answer to Oedipus (psychoanalysis' dominant story of identity formation), a counterstory that made much more sense as I groped my way toward a PhD.

As a graduate student I was drawn to readings in psychoanalysis, those readings charging my writing and my teaching. Jacques Lacan's idea of "death-work" told me why students (and I) resist, almost violently, the process of revision as a potential death threat to the careful scaffolding of beliefs we want to protect as our selves. Feminist revisions of D. W. Winnicott introduced me to the possibility of creating "potential spaces" that could enable me and my students to revise in classrooms that also value relationships and support. And from Freud himself, who consigned his most disruptive ideas to footnotes, I learned to compose unruly research narratives that seek to expose, not tuck away in footnotes, the troubling subtext of my wishful thinking. In Lacan, Benjamin, Freud, and others I discovered not intrinsic truths about human nature but stories of human relationships that leapt into my writing and my teaching.

Except, that is, for the stumbling block of Oedipus.

A quick sketch of Freud's story of Oedipus for girls: Repudiate the mother and identify with the father; envy your brother's penis and resent the mother for bringing you so ill-equipped into the world, or, if you're a true neurotic who believes you've actually assumed the father's place along with all his parts and power, suffer from castration anxiety until (if you subscribe to Freud's idea of the happy ending for girls) you get a baby, a little penis of your own. While well-adjusted boys are understood to have resolved Oedipal tensions upon reaching adolescence, girls, Freud believed, languish within the triangle indefinitely. "It does little harm to a woman," Freud writes, "if she remains in her feminine Oedipus attitude. . . . She will in that case choose her husband for his paternal characteristics and be ready to recognize his authority" (1949, 77).

Sound outlandish, easy to dismiss? For me, yes and no, for while I loathed this tale, I encountered it repeatedly in narratives of women's academic socialization: Heloise and Abelard, Elizabeth and Descartes, Fuller and Emerson, Dorothea and Mr. Casaubon, Beauvoir and Sartre. Or, more subtly, I encountered stories of women bound to the authority not of a particular mentor but of institutional rituals for constructing discursive authority—the women academics that Gesa Kirsch interviewed for *Women Writing the Academy* who subordinate their voices to those of prominent researchers because these figures are "the only thing I have right now" (1993, 44). Assimilate into established structures or be outside voice and authority: These are the untenable choices (if choices they can be called) with which the Oedipal tale confronts women and girls.

In men's stories of academic socialization too I find a troubling replay of the Oedipal drama, as in *Hunger of Memory* when Richard Rodriguez (1982) rejects his family's "private" language, assimilates into the norms of the dominant culture, and becomes a "public man"—that is, an Oedipal man. For women, however, there's not even the dubious reward of a public self gained through separation and denial. In the Oedipal story the adult woman is merely, Jessica Benjamin writes, a "prize or temptation to regression," "their subordination to man [or to sanctioned forms for academic research] . . . taken for granted" (1988, 6). In resistance, some psychoanalytic feminists have championed the neglected mother of Oedipus, celebrating her assigned traits of oceanic emotion and selfless nurturance. But such an argument continues to pit mother against father, emotion against reason, private relationships against public autonomy, drawing us deeper into the drama of Oedipus.

Hence my delight in finding Moi's story of the infant. This is it, I thought. This is where we should begin when we talk about academic authority: in this prior story that doesn't construct the mother as mute weakness, the father as terrible omnipotence, sons as parricides, daughters as sad neurotics. In this prior story we can learn why Oedipus shouldn't suit us, whether we are women or are men. This is what I thought.

But at the same time Moi's essay promised an exit to Oedipus, it also disturbed me in a way I couldn't name. So I glossed each paragraph, studied how Moi moved from one moment to the next. This is what I found.

Moi begins with a critique of American psychoanalytic feminists, calling their reading of female subjectivity essentialist, unsophisticated. Read: Repudiate the mother. Next, she calls on feminists to turn instead to Lacan. Read: Identify with the father. Her credentials as a Lacanian established, she offers her own reading of Freud's drive theory. Read: Claim the phallus. Finally, after explicating that wondrous tale of the infant, she insists that these ideas are Freud's, not her own. Read: Castration anxiety.

Here, in the essay's latent content, is why I was so troubled. The essay's form didn't show a writer groping for an always-changing sense of coherence. Instead, the essay's form repeated the story of Oedipus and all its pathologizing effects for women. More, the essay's traditional academic form suggested that in Oedipus we have a drama not only about the formation of identity in general but of academic identity in particular.

When Oedipus Writes a Dissertation

When I sat down to draft my dissertation in 1994, I felt I was in company of a great many feminist scholars who were voicing restlessness with the idea that, as Jessica Benjamin puts it, "we grow *out of* relationships rather than becoming more active and sovereign *within* them" (1988, 18). These feminists pointed me toward my dissertation, where, inspired particularly by Moi's essay, I wanted to examine acts of revision within that drive toward different kinds of coherence that are constantly undone and opened up by a life's, a society's, restless rhythms. By the time I sat down to draft, I had not only a plan but such a strong sense I had so much to say, the dissertation seemed already written, its future (if I could just make a schedule, stick to it) something like glorious.

Surrounding my desk with the books and articles I would draw on for support, I began:

> Revision, a popular topic among writing teachers during the 70s and 80s, is rarely mentioned these days in composition's professional discourse, perhaps because, as John Trimbur writes. . . .

Huh?

Block-deleting, I tried again:

> Recently, compositionists with a commitment to feminism have worked to complicate our theories of composing through introducing gender as a category of difference and through constructing feminist models for writing instruction. Left largely unexamined, however, is the idea of revision and how feminism might be brought to bear. . . .

There it was a second time, stronger than before: the voice of one whose authority depends on detailing how all prior voices are naive, unsophisticated, a bunch of castrated mothers.

This is not a stance I believe in, and this was precisely the attitude toward my discipline's foremothers and current voices that I did not want my dissertation to take. I didn't consider, though, how this is also a stance that the Oedipal tale—with its insistence on individuation created through separation and denial—has prepared for academic writers in advance. I didn't consider how very easy it is to step into such a position and call it the only position available. Freud's story was fitting me all too well: Oedipus was sitting down to write a dissertation.

I tell this story because I'm convinced that others' stories of the dissertation begin in much the same way—with struggle against or acquiescence to a larger narrative of academic socialization. Dissertations in composition and rhetoric have their manifest content—about revision, collaboration, critical pedagogy. They also have their latent content, whispering their stories of how we get credentialed and how the discipline is being reconstituted. We need to engage with that repressed text and the Oedipal imperatives that underwrite it if we're to consider anew the discipline our dissertations create. I also want to revisit that latent content because I think it can tell us that the dominant narrative of academic socialization is just that: a construction whose workings we can examine. When we resist seeing stories of education as the way it must be, when we resist seeing a tale like Oedipus as a statement of what's essentially true about an individual's psyche or about Western history, we can begin to examine how these stories are made, according to what narrative devices.

Because time—how to understand my present, how to predict my future—was so central to my concerns as a graduate student, I want to focus particularly on devices of time. Specifically, I'll examine how dominant stories of academic socialization and the Oedipal tale are together such powerful narratives because they understand the future as knowable, time as closed, and thus operate according to the device of foreshadowing. A meditation on foreshadowing—its presentation of a seductively clear vision of the future, its attempt in both psychoanalytic and academic settings to relieve us of having to grapple with present-moment relationships—can complicate how we tell stories of dissertation-writing and advising. Instead of falling into dichotomous arguments about writer's desires versus reader's expectations, the dissertation as a "hoop" versus the dissertation as a real occasion for writing, we can instead examine how foreshadowing is present in all these formulations. We can examine too what the problems of that narrative device may be, the many questions about the future it works to deny.

At the same time, we can turn to a less familiar narrative practice called *sideshadowing*, one that can disrupt and alter the meaning of the Oedipal tale, disrupt and alter the dissertation scene as well. Like foreshadowing, sideshadowing is a way of shaping and understanding history and time. In contrast to foreshadowing, however, sideshadowing seeks to loosen that lid on a sealed-tight future. It urges writers to self-consciously move—even if only for ten minutes or for five—from writing *as if* the future is fixed to wondering *what if* it is not.

With these phrases—writing *as if,* writing *what if*—I'm not offering a restatement of the familiar "writing to show you know" versus "writing to know" (Moffett 1994, 18). Instead, I want to invoke two tendencies in language that are simultaneously present in any moment of writing—what Mikhail Bakhtin (1981) calls centripetal and centrifugal forces, the push toward unification, the pull toward diversification. I also want to suggest two competing stances about time that likewise could be called into operation: the stance produced by foreshadowing, telling us to write *as if* the future were known; the stance produced by sideshadowing, telling us to pause, ask *what if* and wonder about the other possible futures a present moment may hold. Through raising *what if* questions, the practice of sideshadowing doesn't seek to replace one future with another, this story with that, the tale of the infant supplanting that of Oedipus. Instead, sideshadowing multiplies stories, multiplies futures, and thus confronts writers with the complexities of commitment.

On Foreshadowing, or Writing *As If*

I take this term *sideshadowing* from Bakhtinian theorist Gary Saul Morson (1994), who considers its power to counter narrative inevitability in novels. First, though, a look at the much more familiar practice of foreshadowing.

Foreshadowing, Morson writes, "projects onto the present a shadow from the future" and thus gives the future the appearance of the preordained (9). It places the present moment in service to the future it proclaims while draining the present of other possibilities. In a single moment foreshadowing both predicts and confirms. Thus my first attempt at dissertation drafting was a collection of thesis statements foreshadowing the dissertation to come; had I continued to write from those statements, I'd have written to confirm them and the future they anticipated. My own statements a moment ago—"I want to revisit that latent content . . . ," "I want to focus particularly on . . ."—also rely on foreshadowing, predicting and confirming the essay to come.

Composition's narratives of academic socialization from the 1980s—narratives of how students must be gently invited into or aggressively confronted with academic conventions—were also written through the narrative device of foreshadowing, and subsequent critiques of those narratives—against the conservative mission of assimilation (Mortensen and Kirsch 1993); against the stress on the centralizing forces within a discourse community without concomitant attention to forces of diversification and change (Cooper 1994); against defining composition as a field that uncritically supports how academic writing gets done (Bartholomae 1996)—can be read as critiques of such foreshadowing. By giving the future that appearance of the preordained, Morson writes, foreshadowing robs the present of its "eventness," its "surprisingness";

the present moment becomes only a step toward that future. When we take issue with assimilationist constructions of academic socialization, we take issue with this loss of eventness, with this attempt to leapfrog past the complexities of an academic text in its moments of becoming.

Of course I want to argue for restoring eventness to dissertation scenes as well. I want to demonstrate how we can extend our critiques of academic socialization/Oedipalization into this rhetorical scene. Yet I can't simply reject the history-shaping allure of foreshadowing. I have to confront my instant acquiescence to the Oedipal tale I thought I had no truck with. What's so enthralling about this device of foreshadowing in Oedipus and stories of learning to write? Why would we submit so readily to this robbery of eventness and surprise?

I find one possible answer when I consider that through foreshadowing we have not so much a robbery as an exchange: an exchange of the capacity to be surprised (and also confused, uncertain, without direction) for the capacity to feel certain and sure, our sense of self and direction not just confirmed but *affirmed.* Viewing Oedipus as a tale "every child is destined to pass through" (1949, 69), Freud could predict and confirm a patient's particular illness. Freud could not see other stories through which we might read and interpret a life—a profound and, particularly for women, consequential loss—but through Oedipus there was also for Freud a gain as his patients' stories took on coherence and meaning. Similarly, when we read and respond to students' text through the predictive narrative of necessary assimilation, we cannot see other stories through which we might read and interpret—a profound and consequential loss. But there's gain too as a stack of drafts takes on shape, making us feel that yes, these are students we can converse with, think with, understand.

Foreshadowing also tries to affirm that we are pursuing a responsible course of action: "I have a responsibility to teach my students the conventions"; "I'm responsible for ensuring that my doctoral students write a solid, get-a-job dissertation"; "It's my responsibility to show I really know the field, really know my stuff." In every conversation I can think of in which the question of diversifying academic writing has come up, at least one person has voiced a conversation-stopping assertion of responsibility. A few years back, a feminist scholar visited my campus to talk about her work in the erotics of writing and teaching. Asked how she approaches the teaching of writing, she replied, "I teach them the rules of the academic essay. They can't get away with writing like me." Similarly, when an established scholar was asked at a conference how others might follow her lead in publishing first-person essays in journals like *College English,* she shook her head. "They won't let you," she said. "It would be irresponsible for me to suggest otherwise. You have to get to where I am, and then you can write however you want."

In both cases, I believe, these scholars felt they were offering responsible replies. But in both cases their replies also deflected responsibility elsewhere: onto journal editors and classroom professors constructed as tradition-bound. Both speak *as if* they are certain of the requirements of these other professors and journal editors (*but what if they are not*?). Both speak *as if* they themselves have no investment in these norms they are bound to uphold (*but what if they do*?). Most disturbing to me, they speak *as if* they are indeed castrated mothers who must redirect sons and daughters away from attachment to their bodies of work, and they speak *as if,* given a little more power, they really would encourage experimentation in their students' texts (*but what if they would not*?).

Statements of obligation can prevent us from examining our own complicity in existing arrangements and from wondering whether these really *are* the existing arrangements across classrooms and across disciplinary lines. Such statements prevent us from interrogating the comfort we take in the idea of closed time, certain outcomes, nameable constraints, a predetermined story through which to write so we can be done with all questions of what that writing might mean. These assertions of responsibility actually turn us away from a responsible assessment of present-time relationships, turn us instead toward the boot-strap individualism that underwrites composition's dominant story of academic socialization and psychoanalysis's Oedipal story of development both: This child, like all children before, must negotiate and come through these Oedipal tensions alone; he, outside and heroically struggling, must learn to write like us; she must get where I am the hard way. Meanwhile, a whole host of responsible questions never come up: What are the implications of this future-in-the-making? What's my investment in this future? What are the other futures this particular future, and my support of it, may foreclose?

On Sideshadowing or Writing *What If*?

These are the questions posed by the narrative practice of sideshadowing. Sideshadowing doesn't ignore social realities nor supplant the allure of foreshadowing and the material conditions that make working toward a certain future necessary. But the practice of sideshadowing does ask us to consider that we too frequently commit ourselves to a course of action without really examining the present moment. Sideshadowing attempts to redirect our attention to the present moment, its unexamined surplus. As Morson writes, sideshadowing

> projects—from the "side"—the shadow of an alternative present. It allows us to see what might have been and therefore changes our view of what is . . . time itself becomes a succession not just of points of actuality but also of fields of possibility. (1994, 11–12)

Sideshadowing doesn't replace one storyline with another. Both the story of Oedipus and the story of the infant are within the "fields of possibility"; neither can assert itself as *the* "point of actuality." Neither is sideshadowing a part of a utopian project to find the single correct theory that promises a restful, question-free future. Utopianism, as Morson points out, very much relies on the device of foreshadowing, viewing the present moment and its participants as "mere raw material for the great time to come" (17). In contrast, sideshadowing asks us to imagine the world "as an eventful process capable of leading to many diverse futures" (42). Instead of telling *the* story, sideshadowing seeks to multiply the stories that can be told at any given moment. It seeks to place our certainty about any of these stories in profound tension with our awareness of the claims of the others. "Sideshadows," Morson writes, "conjure the ghostly presence of might-have-beens or might-bes" (118).

We can find, if we know what we're looking for, stories of academic becoming that counter foreshadowing, disrupt narrative determinism, and reintroduce eventness to the scene of writing. From the field of philosophy, for instance, Michele Le Dœuff recounts the "methodological subjectivism" of feminist consciousness-raising groups that sideshadowed, disrupted, and revised her thinking not only about method in philosophy but also the very (masculinist) definition of philosophers as "people who know absolutely what they are saying" and whose work "has no hidden content which might have escaped the author" (1991, 166). Le Dœuff's account is very much about becoming a philosopher, about establishing a commitment to her chosen discipline, but it's a commitment worked at through sideshadows, through simultaneously questioning what this commitment means and what this profession can be.

In composition I find the reinterpretive potential of sideshadowing when Min-Zhan Lu (1994) asks that students look again at an apparent "error" in a draft and resist correction long enough to consider how that moment in the text is also meaningful. Working *within* the tension between official and alternative discursive codes, Lu's students imagine multiple readings of and futures for this moment, the multiple consequences for each. Such a classroom practice isn't fostering uncritical acceptance of all expression. Quite the opposite: It reopens what would otherwise be an entirely uncritical acceptance of convention as teacher and students confront a point of actuality—the official norms of written academic English—and struggle to relocate that point of actuality within a field of other readings.

Neither Le Dœuff nor Lu suggests the utopian wish of reaching a restful, question-free future. Instead, each demonstrates how the future is complicated through the discovery of a present-moment surplus. Yes, disciplinary and generic constraints are there, telling a writer, "You have to, indeed you want to, project yourself into a place of at-homeness within this pre-existing code." Yes, the story of Oedipus is ready to be called onto the stage and produce stick-to-the-outline academic prose. At the same time other possible stories, other possible futures are asking for existence: Margins ask to be glossed, the blank backs of pages wait to be filled.

Sideshadowing the Dissertation

Since how much sideshadowing a writer can do very much depends on material conditions and institutional realities, I want to end with ways in which dissertation writers and advisors can work together to create eventness and surprise.

Sideshadowing Process

We have access to daily sideshadowing practices through composition's process legacy. Or we have such access if we resist that Oedipal urge to declare ourselves "post-process." In composition's process legacy I see practices with the profound potential to keep in simultaneity and tension the pressure to write *as if* with the need to keep asking, *but what if*? In my dissertation, I turned especially to Ann Berthoff, glossing each evening the day's writing, asking *what if* and *what else* and then filling the margins with my responses, my next day's revision work.

Sideshadowing Disciplinarity

Le Dœuff's story of writing between feminism and philosophy tells me, too, that sideshadowing depends not only on a relationship to one's discipline but on forging or maintaining relationships to disciplines, communities, and projects beyond. Working across academic borders introduces us to the "unthought," as Le Dœuff would say, in our own field. This means cultivating what Kenneth Burke (1950) called "perspectives by incongruity"—a doctoral comps reading list, for example, designed not only to orient the student within her or his field but also working for dis-orientation. Through a relationship to voices outside of my field such as Le Dœuff and Benjamin, I was able, the second time I sat down to draft my dissertation's opening chapter, to consider that yes, I did have an argument to make—one that could be made through connection with others.

Sideshadowing Citations

There's a need as well to look again at the relationships we claim as we write, asking "What kind of authority am I trying to create through this name I cite?" and "With whom am I aligning myself and what might the difficulties of that relationship be?" There's the need to ponder, too, the names not cited, the relationships not formed or ignored—and with what possible consequences. Sideshadowing citations can create some surprising juxtapositions, such as Minnie Bruce Pratt and Jacques Lacan invoked together throughout one of my dissertation chapters. These surprising juxtapositions are also eventful, such as Pratt telling me that what Lacan called death-work, the dismantling of beliefs and identifications, needs to be renamed *life-work*. Sideshadowing citations also has the power to change what we think a chapter is all about—static notions of the traditional literature review transformed into the active, genuine work of claiming, examining, questioning, and deepening relationships.

Sideshadowing Authority

If the preceding examples focus primarily on the dissertation writer and how she or he can open up the project-enriching questions and tensions of sideshadowing, I've also realized through my position today the profound need for advisors to do much more than cheer from the sidelines. A dissertation writer can't easily claim an unexpected relationship, take the risk of delving into the complexities of the process, or juxtapose seemingly incongruous perspectives if she or he is working with a committee that discourages (including through its silence) such writing out of bounds. And while for white men there are models of the rebel individualist who takes glee in trashing tradition and turning his back on convention (all ultimately in service to the Oedipal imperative of killing off the father so that one may assume his place and exert authority over others in turn), there are few such models for women (and for men who seek an alternative or who are excluded from the models of a Kerouac or Bukowski). Instead, as I find in Kirsch's (1993) interviews with women academics, the lesson women are most commonly taught through their academic apprenticeships is that they'll be rewarded for working within tradition, particularly in the form of praise for being such careful readers.

Dissertation writers should not be called on alone to intervene in such a lesson (one reinforcing that a woman can get through the Oedipal triangle only by moving into a permanent position of subordination). Dissertation committee members also must participate. For me that's meant deliberately examining my notions of who in the advising relationship has knowledge and authority. It's meant making sure that each time I work with a writer on a project, we figure out first the knowledge and commitments we're *both* bringing to the relationship—for instance, my knowledge of literacy studies coming together with a master's student's knowledge of post-NAFTA geopolitical realities. In such a relationship who advises whom constantly shifts. How to relish such shifts is what I learned from my own dissertation advisors, who welcomed my ventures into new theoretical realms and who taught me that real advising begins with the admission of "I don't know . . ." followed by "Tell me" and "I need to learn about this too."

Sideshadowing Oedipus

Despite all I've suggested, the Oedipal story of academic socialization will continue to pose difficulty unless we examine our tacit acceptance of the tale's premises, particularly the narcissism it is designed to provide a solution to. Consider: When a friend tells me in exhaustion and despair of her committee's relentless challenges to her dissertation chapter drafts—challenges, made in the name of rigor, that have dragged on now for nearly three years—I think (it doesn't matter that I should know better) that rigor is what my committee let me sidestep. Consider too: After completing her multigenre, multilingual thesis, the master's student I mentioned above said she couldn't shake the sense that I and other committee members had let her do a project that wouldn't have been "allowed" anywhere else—this despite her being able to name a long list of border theorists who also blur boundaries between poetics and rhetoric and between languages and voice registers.

The *in loco parentis* relationships that, as John Trimbur (2000) argues, underwrite first-year writing classrooms also underwrite graduate advising relationships, and they will continue to do so as long as we leave the Freudian model of the white, middle-class family unexamined. In this model, the advisor is either the stern father who constantly calls his advisee/child into account or the indulgent mother who protects her advisee/child from such "rigor." What this strong daddy/soft mommy construction erases is the hard work I engaged in as a dissertation writer to enter disciplinary conversations from a direction different from that of my advisors and the work of my advisors to challenge me not by addressing me as an unruly child but as a fully grown-up colleague. What the Freudian family model erases is the hard work of the master's student to create a multidisciplinary project that would speak across academic borders—and that, when it came to the thesis defense, I and one other committee member who was likewise Anglo and non-Spanish-speaking had to be accountable for our reading strategies. If the Oedipal story of advisor-writer relationships is left unexposed, these much more dynamic and instructive relationships are erased even by those who experienced and grew within them. What we are left with is the uneasy sense we must be overly mothered children not permitted to grow up. It doesn't matter how much evidence we can amass to the contrary—our belief that the Oedipal narrative is a necessary intervention in infantile narcissism is that ingrained.

What can we do? We can counter that speech-stopping word *rigor* with a complex and nuanced understanding of the word *relationship*. *Relationship* is a word I've stressed throughout this chapter because there we have the most potent sideshadow to the Oedipal tale, reminding us that in sideshadowing Oedipus, we're not embracing narcissism and denying reality but instead embracing relationship, involvement, an intersubjective understanding of academic research, writing, and advising that thoroughly troubles and takes us beyond the static family relationships of Freud. When we defend the Oedipal imperatives of denial, separation, and assimilation, saying that otherwise we or our advisees will be awash in infantile narcissism, we actually voice (as Benjamin writes) a "nostalgia for old forms of authority and morality" (1988, 129) and an allegiance to conservative, paternalistic family values that have justified the subordination of people by gender, race, sexuality, and class at home, at work, and in the academy.

In fact, since Freud, research into the pre-Oedipal phase—by Jessica Benjamin, D. W. Winnicott, Daniel Stern, and many others, including Toril Moi, with whom my chapter began—can tell us that this primary narcissism, this state of presocialization and predifferentiation we seem to so greatly fear, does not exist, not as Freud believed. Instead, we are primed from the beginning for a dance between self and other, fusion and separation, sameness and difference, foreshadows and sideshadows—a dance that shouldn't end at the age of four or eighteen or with the penning of a dissertation's first paragraph.

Chapter Five

Dissertation Writing and Advising in a Postmodern Age

Catherine G. Latterell and Cynthia L. Selfe

With other contributors to this collection, we contend that the field of composition has paid inadequate attention to the forces acting on PhD candidates and their advisors. We maintain as well that the frameworks currently used to understand this writer-advisor relationship also need exploration and revision. Although our profession has made dramatic strides in rethinking the demands associated with many common composition tasks—and the postmodern contexts that lend new shape and complexity to these demands—we have done very little to bring these understandings to bear on the specific demands involved in working on a dissertation project.

Our lack of attention to these demands becomes more puzzling when we recognize that what takes place between PhD candidates and their advisors will influence one of the most important pieces of writing—and will prove to be one of the most important working relationships—in an academic's life. For many scholars, dissertation writing represents the penultimate moment of acceptance and identification. With so much at stake, it should not surprise us to find different understandings of disciplines and literacies bumping up against each other, requiring negotiation. In this essay, we examine and situate the roles and responsibilities of faculty advisors—especially as these have been shaped by the demands of inter- and multi-disciplinarity that characterize composition studies in the postmodern age. We also try to provide readers some sense of how faculty responses affect students who are engaged in writing their dissertations.

As students, we experience the task of writing a dissertation only once; as faculty advisors, however, we relive the process again and again, and each time we do, we are given another chance to define the advising relationship through a negotiation with the students who share our lives. Many of this collection's chapters describe how students writing dissertations need to negotiate a new and increasingly complex set of postmodern identities. This essay suggests that advisors, too, need to rethink models for advising—particularly when operating within a field that is increasingly informed by the cross-disciplinary work. We begin with examples from a set of advising practices identified in the graduate program in Rhetoric and Technical Communication at Michigan Technological University in a very specific time, the mid-1990s. We believe that the challenges of this time and place can provide a fruitful ground for scholars to begin rethinking the tasks of writing and advising multi- or interdisciplinary dissertations.

Why Michigan Tech? The first answer is obvious: This is where Kate earned her degree in 1996 and where Cindy, her advisor, has served on the faculty for twenty-one years. Second, because Michigan Tech's doctoral program is in a humanities department composed of some eighteen disciplines, this program is fundamentally defined by its multi- or interdisciplinary character. Although it lacks one kind of defining tension within many English departments—the literature, creative writing, and composition tug-of-war—this humanities department faces another set of tensions: how dissertation writers and faculty advisors negotiate what dissertations look like when such projects draw on the intellectual traditions and practices of multiple disciplines. As we will discuss, whether in meetings, graduate seminars, or hallway conversations, such negotiations do not remain in the background but instead play central roles in the program. In the first part of our essay, we describe how people in this program reflected on the question central to any dissertation relationship (one with special relevance in the multidisciplinary setting): How do we define the nature of this dissertation? In the second part, we turn to the next logical question: How do advisors and writers in multi- or interdisciplinary contexts define their roles and responsibilities?

Talking Back: The Process and the Nature of Multi- or Interdisciplinarity

The Rhetoric and Technical Communication (RTC) PhD program was initiated in 1989, the first students passing their exams and developing their dissertation proposals three years later. It was at this moment that faculty and students faced the task of determining what would count as a dissertation in a program committed to scholarship extending beyond the conventional boundaries of a single discipline.[1] What had been the familiar and conventional grounds of dissertation-writing—determined in many cases by disciplinary values—became strange territory, available for an intellectual reexamination and remapping.

To deepen our own sense of the challenges that the students and faculty faced at that time—and the insights they had—we interviewed the first dozen PhD graduates, their advisors, and their committee members, as well as faculty members serving then as department chair and director of graduate studies. We also looked back at the dissertation projects of the program's first thirty graduates. Using an open-ended set of interview questions, we wanted to learn: What strategies for directing or advising students did faculty use? What does a multi- or interdisciplinary dissertation look like? How do students and their advisors work in the absence of program models? Emerging from these conversations were concerns about authority, agency, and the roles of advisors—concerns nearly universal to everyone's dissertation-writing experience but perhaps viewed more starkly in this particular context.

Initial dissertations were necessarily experimental, blurring both methodological and genre boundaries. One early student's dissertation, for example, drew on media studies, comparative literature, economic theory, and translation theory to develop an analysis of English translations of French film and the cultural and economic influences of Hollywood on the French cinematic industry. The project used historiography as a general methodological approach and was highly narrative in style. Another student used her background in computer science, rhetoric, and cultural studies to examine the rhetoric and representation associated with technology advertisements in modern technical and popular publications. A third student applied his background in bodybuilding to the intersection of psychoanalytic theory and feminist theory to write a dissertation that reexamined Freud's physiological psychology. Kate's own dissertation blended interpretative and qualitative research methods to examine current trends in composition and rhetoric teaching assistant education programs. On any given dissertation committee, faculty might represent an area in which they had received formal training in graduate school, an area in which they had developed a recent interest and had begun to publish in, or an area in which they had no training or publications, but were willing to read and study along with students.

While there was general satisfaction regarding the coursework and the comprehensive exams, faculty did not necessarily share a common vision of what dissertations should look like. In part, the faculty's understandings of dissertations were determined by their own histories and disciplinary education. Some scholars at Michigan Tech maintained an allegiance to conventional forms of modernist textual examination, others to empirical methodologies growing out of the social sciences, and still others to interpretive and theoretical analyses informed by postmodern social theory. As one department chair stated during this early period, "Dissertations that are multidisciplinary or interdisciplinary are challenges in large part because it's difficult to figure out the methodology and to bring scholars together who can tolerate others' approaches." The real challenge for this program, then, quickly focused on the question, "What does it mean to call a dissertation 'interdisciplinary'?" The following characterizes two responses we heard to this question—both shaping how faculty advisors define their responsibilities to the dissertating student and to their disciplinary field(s).

The first response we will refer to as *multidisciplinary*, although colleagues responding to our questions did not necessarily make such a distinction. Faculty with this view held that a multidisciplinary dissertation should draw substantially from two or more separate and distinct fields in order to address one overarching question and that this dissertation's methodological approaches should be vetted by specialist readers in these separate fields. Additionally, these faculty felt that a multidisciplinary dissertation should position graduates for joint appointments or students with the option of applying for jobs in two or more distinct fields, each with its own sets of standards, methods, canonical texts, and intellectual foci. A dissertation was not multidisciplinary, one faculty member maintained, if it insisted on "primarily addressing issues and concerns in a single field," or if it was "aimed at readers in that field."

A second sense of disciplinarity we will refer to as *interdisciplinary*. Faculty with this point of view generally assumed the audience for a dissertation to be readers in a single field that exists in the intersections of many fields. As one faculty member put it, "Composition studies is a mix of disciplines and genres already. The best advice I can give students working in interdisciplinary studies is to be honest to all disciplines by keeping up with every discipline they touch on. Composition studies is very amenable to blending different genres. It all works." People with this viewpoint believed in weaving together the threads of various disciplines to form new research approaches not necessarily attached to any one traditional disciplinary design, reading texts that resisted the boundaries of conventionally defined fields, acknowledging and combining standards from multiple disciplines, and avoiding false claims of mastery of any one field. This practice did not necessarily recognize disciplines as distinct entities and did not necessarily acknowledge methodologies or texts or intellectual topics as belonging to any one field. One graduate explained, "My committee chair guided me as I began to make connections among social theories, technology criticism, and literacy and writing. The melding of these disciplines was not difficult; they came together naturally." Another, whose work relied on linguistics, composition, education, and gender studies, said, "I didn't have much negotiating to do since all the fields intersected neatly in the social sciences."

The implications of these two definitions of disciplinary research for dissertation projects became the focus of our interviews with a small number of the faculty and past students. *Multidisciplinary* research, which required the writer to be equally knowledgeable in several disciplines and to speak equally to multiple specialist audiences, seemed more time intensive. Several former students told us they found that material conditions such as funding deadlines precluded their involvement in multidisciplinary research projects. *Interdisciplinary* research, in contrast, gave some graduate students room to mix questions and insights from different fields of study,[2] though, understandably, it did not always yield a comfortable position for a dissertation writer. As one graduate put it, "I'm not sure all my committee members were happy with that approach, but I think they were willing to go with it and see what happened."

Nor was it always a comfortable position for the faculty who candidly admitted that attitudes in the department ranged from the belief that the practices and texts of specific disciplines were the property of specialists in those disciplines to a belief that disciplinary boundaries were outdated and that individual scholars, sometimes with little exposure to the history and values of a discipline, could freely borrow from several disciplines to create new areas of study. For faculty and students favoring a multidisciplinary approach, interdisciplinarity raised the threat of being colonized by core areas within the graduate program, particularly composition and rhetoric, which seemed too willing to use the approaches of various fields without adequate concern for their origins. However, for other faculty and students, supporting an interdisciplinary approach meant viewing the enterprise as a collaborative learning and teaching experience. Although some faculty surmised that those in traditional fields—language, philosophy, linguistics, communications—would be most committed to multidisciplinary dissertations while those in less traditional fields would be more comfortable with interdisciplinarity, this was not borne out in our interviews. Faculty and students in technical communication and composition studies, for example, held both points of view about the nature of disciplinarity, as did scholars in linguistics, philosophy, languages, and cultural studies.

During our conversations with faculty advisors, one outlined the two very different perspectives on disciplinarity that existed within the department:

> We must develop a more restricted definition of what it means to produce interdisciplinary dissertations . . . if we are to protect against students and faculty mining the resources of other fields in the name of interdisciplinarity. If students or faculty want to claim interdisciplinarity, then they ought to set up structures that ensure equality among fields.
>
> There are people (Stanley Fish comes to mind) who think interdisciplinarity is an impossibility. One field is always appropriated by another. I am not so cynical. If the dissertation is meant for diverse audiences, then the chair has to make sure that the student is given every opportunity to write in diverse ways and be in touch with diverse resources.

As suggested in the above, faculty frequently described serving simultaneously as mentors and coaches for students, researchers and gatekeepers for their disciplines, and departmental citizens as they faced decisions about who could teach specific courses and about what areas faculty could represent on a dissertation committee.

Faculty concerns about disciplinarity often coalesced around the placement of students in the job market and the importance of students being able to claim disciplinary expertise. Most faculty serving as dissertation chairs worried—and still worry—about how to help students approach their chosen topic in ways that would be acceptable to all committee members and result in dissertations that would serve students well upon graduation. Some faculty members also worried about students feeling overwhelmed by the responsibility of representing multiple fields well in their dissertations, and many worried about students trying to reconcile different approaches—differing methodologies and texts—when faculty themselves couldn't do so. One advisor wrote:

> Maybe what we need to do is to make students aware of the potential richness of interdisciplinarity as well as the realities of disciplinarity. Graduate students need to write a dissertation within a limited period of time, and they hope that doing so will lead to employment.

Along with this potential richness, several faculty also described their commitment to multi- or interdisciplinarity as "exhausting" with meetings of both comprehensive and dissertation committees often lingering on involved debates.

Three Responses to Dissertation Advising and Writing in a Postmodern Era

We also learned from Michigan Tech that just as faculty simultaneously feel responsibility toward their students, disciplines, and departments, students also experience a mixed set of allegiances: to advisors who are often their primary source of academic assistance, to a discipline or disciplines that serve as sources of intellectual authority, to a profession that they are hoping to enter, and to a department that shapes and is shaped by their scholarly projects. In this fragmented, sometimes contradictory landscape, complicated further by the demands of inter- or multidisciplinary research, how do advisors help doctoral candidates acquire the authority necessary to deal—or to break—with traditional disciplinary conventions?

At Michigan Tech and at the twenty or more other doctoral programs we've worked with or visited, we have observed three very different kinds of student-advisor relationships forming around multi- or interdisciplinary dissertation projects. Though these relationships do not describe the universe of advisor-student relationships and though they aren't always clearly distinguishable from one another, they do represent typical responses to the complex challenges of multi- or interdisciplinarity.

Relationship 1: Advising as Empire Building

The first and most typical student-advisor relationship, which forms characteristically around multidisciplinary dissertations, relies on a territorial imperative to define how advisors derive their authority to direct doctoral candidates.

Here, advisors consider their primary responsibility to the scholarly values of their disciplinary fields; they seek to protect their disciplinary turf and increase its intellectual visibility by sponsoring graduate students who will carry forward what the field deems appropriate research agendas. Often advisors taking this approach feel the weight of well-established disciplinary standards and maintain that such standards must be honored. Whether the field of study is more classical, like history of rhetoric, or more hip, like cultural studies, these standards are described as the discipline's lifeblood. The advisor often maintains a high degree of control, serving as the primary arbiter of truth for the doctoral candidate. Such advisors believe they are acting in students' best interests by ensuring that they will be able to claim true disciplinary specialization. It may also be that the turf these faculty are protecting is in their own departments, given that most departments operate in a climate of limited resources. The strength of this approach is that students head into their own careers with an extensive understanding of their field's knowledge base as that base exists both currently and historically. At the same time, such a view can limit students' ability to think along routes that do not follow typical disciplinary directions and can create a damaging departmental atmosphere in which students are less individuals than pawns in battles for control.

Relationship 2: Advising as Cheerleading

The second kind of student-advisor relationship, forming characteristically around interdisciplinary dissertation projects, shifts responsibility from the advisor to the student, downplaying or denying the advisor's disciplinary authority. Advisors may position student writers as the primary or even sole driving force behind a dissertation, defining their own responsibility primarily as a cheerleader who protects students' rights to their own agenda. While for some advisors this may be akin to a sink-or-swim lesson, this relationship is often founded on a suspicion of disciplinary authority. With their belief in the provisional and positional nature of disciplinary knowledge, these advisors try to avoid imposing one set of disciplinary standards on students—or in a variation of this model, an advisor may request that all methodologies and perspectives be given equal weight. The strength of this approach, of course, is the breadth of possibilities that it provides as multiple fields, methods, and theoretical positions become fair game for a dissertation writer. Its weakness is that it feeds the nihilism associated with postmodern theory and that its very technique of nondirectiveness can be a controlling response, especially for students working on multi- or interdisciplinary dissertations. Faced with a lack of direction from an advisor—and shaky confidence in their own abilities—students often fall back on conventional and well-established epistemological perspectives from the discipline or disciplines they have come to know best in order to produce a safe and acceptable dissertation.

Relationship 3: Advising/Writing as Responsibility for the Postmodern Other

The best advisor-student relationships we have seen involve redefining the conventional notions of authority (or power) from which both parties operate in connection with multi- or interdisciplinary projects. In an intellectual world characterized by dizzying speed, expansion, and multiplicity, a world challenged by the disappearance of conventional anchors for authority, individuals in these relationships seem to recognize that power (in the form of knowledge) is not a possession advisors hand down to students. Instead, they understand that power exists within complex sets of social relations and as a result of individual interactions that construct a field of possibilities for responsiveness. Michel Foucault (1983) provides understanding of such relationships when he argues that power circulates as people interact with each other. Within these relationships, power is articulated on a continual basis through the actions of individuals, which in turn influence other people's action. He writes:

> A power relationship can only be articulated on the basis of two elements . . . that "the other" (the one over whom power is exercised) be thoroughly recognized and maintained to the very end as a person who acts; and that, faced with a relationship of power, a whole field of responses, reactions, results, and possible inventions may open up. (220)

In other words, both advisors and students create, through their relationship, a field of social possibilities. Within this field, both exert agency—a "permanent provocation" of wills (222)—to define questions and seek answers. Put another way, good advising/writing relationships remain dynamic—advisor and student both taking turns questioning, listening, responding, and asking, "What does this mean?" as dissertation planning, researching, and writing takes new turns.

Thus, a third approach to the question of how advisors might see their role in a postmodern climate relies on an ethic of care or responsibility for the other that permits a responsive—even inventive—relationship among committee, student, and research agenda. Marilyn Cooper (1997, 1999), whose writing about postmodern ethics relies on the work of Zygmunt Bauman and Emmanuel Levinas, describes what this stance might involve: "'Sharing' power is not a matter of giving up something you have but rather of deciding what you want to do in any given situation and being conscious of taking responsibility for how what you do affects others" (149). Here, how advisors respond to doctoral students—and to colleagues who make up their professional research communities and their departmental programs—is not rule-based but shaped fundamentally by a responsiveness to and for others. When we base relations on this ethic, Cooper writes, we accept Levinas' argument that our capacity to be responsible for the other establishes our subjectivity:

> Being responsible thus is not a matter of suppressing one's "natural" self-interestedness in favor of an effort to be good or to try to follow the rules but

> rather a fundamental impulse to be an individual agent, to be someone whose existence makes a difference. (151)

Such a postmodern ethic of responsibility manifests itself in a student-advisor relationship in a number of ways, such as in the dialogue among committee members and with a doctoral student. Imagine (or recall from your own experience) meetings with committee members and students over dissertation research. Who speaks and who listens in such a meeting? Who questions and who answers? Material circumstances and institutional pressures that position committee members as authorities could encourage advisors to offer and writers to take expeditious answers, but those guided by an ethic of responsibility to and for others resist such urges. One characteristic, then, of this perspective is advisors' and writers' willingness to slow down, to resist playing it safe so they might work together to imagine the multiple next moves a dissertator might make, always discussing what could be at stake for the student, the research, and for the committee.

Another characteristic of this perspective is that while advisors acknowledge preestablished disciplinary standards, they are not altogether constrained by them because, as Cooper suggests, they recognize that adherence to such standards will not necessarily help students build new connections within their doctoral research or "take responsibility for their own positions" (157). Nor do advisors working in such a relationship leave students to their own devices when making decisions. Rather, they approach a multi- or interdisciplinary dissertation project as a teaching and learning experience for which both the advisor and the student will take responsibility because they are engaged in a relationship characterized by mutual care.

When both advisor and writer take responsibility for each other's success in such a project, they ask each other questions, seek each other's advice, respect and value each other's difference, and deal with tensions in ways that promote creative and nontraditional responses to the problems of research and writing. We don't mean to make things sound simple—such relationships require working against the grain of a tradition that seems based on common sense and against the understandable urge to follow the path of least resistance.

In Conclusion

When we asked graduates how their multi- or interdisciplinary dissertations positioned them after they had defended, their reports were mixed. Several graduates' responses are best illustrated by one who wrote that his interdisciplinary scholarship "has allowed me to make interdisciplinary connections which would not have been possible in the past." Another graduate student reported, "I think I'm perceived as out-of-bounds and negative to the conservative folks [in my field] and as forward-thinking to others." A third graduate voiced what was also a common concern: Her interdisciplinary dissertation helped her publish her work in a number of forums but also put her "in a more difficult position on the job market."

Overall, the first graduates of Michigan Tech's doctoral program echoed what their advisors had said: Multi- and interdisciplinary work allows them to pursue questions that extend beyond the conventional borders of a single discipline; such work is also exhausting and not without career risks. Simply stating that at least 90 percent hold jobs in higher education oversimplifies the career and life paths of program graduates. The variety of positions these individuals now hold reveals much more: the director of a center for teaching and technological innovation at a well-known engineering college; the head of a reference and instructional services group in the library of a technological university; a tenure-track faculty member in the English department of a large state university; the director of a writing center.

As we said in the introduction, we experience writing a dissertation only once; as faculty, however, we relive the process, and thus we are given an opportunity to contemplate anew the advising relationships we negotiate with students. In taking responsibility for such matters, we hope to use the three models of advisor-student relationships described in this chapter as a starting point for continued reflection. We hope that both faculty and students working on multi- and interdisciplinary projects become increasingly conscious of the ways in which they work with, respond to, and take responsibility for each other. This kind of micropolitics, we believe, can make a real difference in the lives of both students and faculty, even if institutionalized practices change more slowly.

End Notes

1. The RTC program grew out of a belief that, in order to prepare faculty to teach in an increasingly global marketplace, in new electronic environments, and in multiplying and divergent cultural situations, a program must draw on a number of disciplinary knowledge bases, including composition studies, technology studies, visual studies, communication, and psychology.

2. Just as faculty in this program have wide-ranging disciplinary backgrounds, so do the graduate students. The first PhD graduate from this program, Johndan Johnson-Eilola, majored as an undergraduate in geological engineering and considered switching his major to computer science before focusing on technical communication. His dissertation, "Nostalgic Angels: Reconsidering Hypertext Writing," was informed by work in technology studies, education, computer science, cultural studies, communication, composition studies, social theory, and postmodern theory. On his dissertation committee were faculty members with backgrounds in physics, composition, technology studies, and linguistics.

Chapter Six

Mothers, Spinsters, Othermothers

Metaphors for Women Mentors and Their Students

Joy Ritchie, Kate Ronald, and Hephzibah Roskelly

Kate: Have you ever listened to dissertation drafts over the phone? Now, that's the worst kind of mentoring because you can't do anything but reinforce and stroke. Or I spend too much time talking about what might be written rather than reading drafts. One of my main roles seems to be the believer, the one who can find the thread of the idea among all that talk.

Hepsie: Now I realize that's part of our job, but it's the strokiness that bothers me. I want people to be grown-up. I really admire their work, and if they don't begin with that situation of trust when they write a dissertation, I can't give it to them by keeping on shoring them up.

Joy: I was thinking last night of the kinds of roles my students and I are placed in; they become the never-grateful-enough daughter or son, the usurping, all-consuming child who wants to be at the breast all the time. Or the rebellious child who doesn't want our words of wisdom. And we become the too distant or distracted mother, or the domineering, overcontrolling mother.

Kate: But we're cast into nurturing roles all the time. Or we take them on, seek them out. And it's difficult to resist that role, especially when the profession can be so brutal.

We talk to each other about our work with graduate students all the time. We use this talk to commiserate about the burden of caring for writers who are at one of the most stressful points of their lives. We also use this talk to help each other figure out our roles as directors, particularly the charged role of mother we all too often fit within, not only because our students want to be mothered but also because we want to change the patriarchal terms of academic accomplishment and success. As feminists in composition and as advocates of critical pedagogy, we push against traditional rites of academic initiation, not to eliminate but to redefine rigor.

Paulo Freire (1996) says the relationship between advisor and dissertation writer should be "agitated," treading a fine line between "warmth" and "serious intellectual discipline" (168–69). For us—as women mentors in a feminized discipline with feminist ways of teaching—that line is sometimes difficult to find. We are too often only agitated. And we're torn between nurturing individuals and getting the work done. We experience constant conflict between taking care of people and carefully taking the profession to new and better places. And so in this essay, we offer a fairly bald discussion of the tensions in our dissertation advising relationships. We want to announce up front that this essay is squarely about the three of us, not a commentary on women in the field; we describe our own ways of working, the traps we've fallen into, the particular tension that we three have experienced in the role of dissertation director.

Then we argue that despite ours and our students' tendencies to see dissertation advising as a mothering relationship, we think two *other* models—spinster and othermother—are more useful both to highlight the dynamics of a woman mentor's position and to push against defining mothering itself within white heterosexist cultural norms. Difficult though they may be to embrace for those of us taught to regard childlessness as a failure, the spinster and othermother, we believe, offer new models for women mentors.

Women as Mentors in a Feminized Space

> The first profession opened to women consisted of the sale of sexual love and was called prostitution; the second, an initiative of nineteenth-century Americans, was a traffic in maternal love and was called pedagogy.
>
> —Redding Sugg (1978),
> *Motherteacher: The Feminization of American Education*

In *A Treatise on Domestic Economy,* written in the mid-nineteenth century, Catherine Beecher (reprint, 1977) outlines her philosophy of the separate but equal roles of men and women in American culture. As educators of the young, mothers have primary responsibility for the society's manners and morals. Beecher even titles one chapter "To Mother Is to Teach." Through the undeniable significance of this role Beecher claims some measure of sex equality, though she didn't believe in women's participation in politics or right to vote. Instead, mothers become the agents of a conservative education, passing on the virtues that the father has demonstrated to be most important. Beecher's *Treatise* might attempt to create a kind of equality through valuing domesticity, as Jane Roland Martin (1989) argues in her work on women's education, but it maintains inequality through the agency of motherhood.

As women in a feminized discipline, we take the dangers of "preserving culture" seriously. So much of what we lose of ourselves as women, thinkers, and writers is lost to preserve an academic culture that hasn't wanted what we as women offered. Despite the great advances women in rhetoric and composition have made, the feminization of the discipline has been well-documented, and more than other academic disciplines, rhetoric and composition continues to be haunted by what Susan Miller (1991) calls the "sad women in the basement." Eileen Schell (1998b), Sue Ellen Holbrooke (1991), and Theresa Enos (1996) have documented the damaging consequences for working conditions, salaries, and status in composition as a result of the identification of teaching with the maternal. And this maternal identification is also perpetuated by stances associated with composition classrooms that attempt to diffuse central, patriarchal authority and to value what Alice Walker calls "everyday use" by attending to process.

These theories and practices affect our positions even as many women have emerged as leaders in rhetoric and composition. As dissertation directors, we are embedded in a long tradition that derives from that most masculine institution, the German university of the nineteenth century, with all of its baggage of disciplining and initiating students into the privileged elite culture of the academy. This model of PhD supervisor, *Doktorvater* in the German university, has been democratized in this country, as David Damrosch (2000) notes, but it still has many traces of the German model in which the solitary student works with a single mentor to produce a work that signals his academic prowess. This mentoring relationship often fails to acknowledge that either the student or the professor has a life outside those institutional roles. Nor does it acknowledge the underlying emotional structures of paternal identification and resistance those roles entail—desire to emulate the father and a parallel desire to reject and or supersede the father's authority. As women coming from positions of less authority (e.g., K–12 teachers, writing center directors, adjunct instructors), we find it easy to be drawn to power and even to out-father the father figure in order to escape the weaker maternal position. Thus we end up preserving the existing academic culture as we mentor our students.

But even when we attempt to be paternal, our authoritative stance is often reread through our female bodies. Our full professor status is always inevitably transfigured to some degree. So rather than being the demanding, rigorous father, we sometimes become the controlling, nagging mother, helping students develop time lines and calendars for getting their work done or coaching them on how to act in front of the father. Or we become the unconditionally loving mother who will always put the best face on the child's work. Or—and this is perhaps the most insidious role—we find ourselves operating as the translator or messenger of the stern father's expectations, all the while implying that we, the mother, are simply trying to mediate the students' desires with those of the paternal institution and profession. Each of these manifestations of mothering remains unsatisfying and somewhat duplicitous.

Mother Love

> Unlike our mothers and our mothers' mothers, we have an unprecedented opportunity outside the home, outside the banal marketplace of getting and spending—in the wonderful world of the academy! Do we therefore believe that we should demonstrate our eternal gratitude (through selfless service) or preserve anachronistic feminine virtues (through selfless service)?
>
> —Susan Gubar (1999), "The Graying of Professor Bombeck"

Despite the problems, we don't simply reject the maternal possibilities in our role as dissertation advisors. This role also has its pleasures and seductions. We have each found great enjoyment in the close daughter/son/friend/colleague relationships we have established with some of our PhD students. The intimacy and honesty that occur when we can acknowledge the realities of our lives make our jobs more tolerable. But one danger of the maternal form of mentoring is that the mother/mentor becomes too invested in the success of the student/child. In addition to the dangers for the student of being exploited by the maternal mentor, the mentor may risk exploitation as well. For many women professors, the increased numbers of PhD students in composition and rhetoric mean that, along with the demands of being tenured professors, many of us have too many graduate students. Cindy Moore (2000) acknowledges this pressure in "A Letter to Women Graduate Students on Mentoring," in which she recounts the story of students applauding her for making herself available to them so much of the time when she knows that this is having a serious impact on her scholarship, her teaching, and her life as the mother of a small child. "What I knew, but didn't say, is that my door is open more often than other doors because I'm an administrator, because I'm required to keep my door open. . . . What I knew, but didn't say, is that I would likely keep my door closed more often, if I could" (149). So although we value the interactions with our students, like many parents, we also need them to leave us alone. In the last five years the three of us have directed over forty dissertation writers, and we simply cannot mother all of them. "Most of us," Theresa Enos (1996) writes, "do not recognize that in the area of teaching and writing we too often participate in a paradigm that threatens our productivity as writers and sometimes our very identities, not to mention our mental health" (30). Mothers, after all, are supposed to put their children first, to think of everyone else's needs before their own. And that's a tempting stance to take, especially, as Gubar reminds us, when we are taught to believe that our privilege requires sacrifice and payback. We resist the "old boy" model of the professor whose own work comes first, whose few office hours are strictly enforced, and who never gets called at home. On the other hand, making room for what Gubar calls the thoroughly tiring work of "bolstering" in one's day, week, career takes its toll.

Kate: I think Hepsie's notion of dealing with the work, not the person, is incredibly interesting because I think my impulse, and I'm not proud of this, has been to go in the opposite direction: You're okay, so now what can we do to make this work okay. And so much of the dissertation is going on at the same time that people are looking for jobs, and they're starting to send things out for publication, and they're getting rejected and feeling bad and going through all the angst that they shouldn't have to go through yet.

Hepsie: I start by telling them that they've had every signal along the way that they are worthy of doing this project. I'm not going to tell you that anymore. What I am going to tell you is what I think of this text, and you can tell me back what you think, but that's what we're going to talk about—the work. We're not going to talk about you. I know that's mean. . . . so if I see them looking particularly woebegone, I might say, "I know I cut out three-fourths of that chapter, but the part that's left is very good," or whatever face to face. But I don't write that out. It's really very far from first-year composition that way. What we do as dissertation mentors is to be good editors.

Joy: But we're not just dealing with the text as an impersonal editor might. We're involved, for better or for worse, in a long-term relationship. (Didn't our mothers all say, "You'll always be my child no matter how old you are?") They're not first-year students, but doctoral candidates, yet even more than undergraduates they're involved in a high-stakes process of constructing professional identities, and as dissertation advisors we're implicated in that, in pathological ways sometimes. That's why even when we're trying to be good editors, it's so fraught with problems.

As we all know, editors are often not motherly. Editors usually do not edit first drafts. Yet each of us has the all-too-frequent experience of finding an eighty-page chapter draft in our mailboxes with the plea, "I just don't know where to cut. Help. I don't know what I'm saying." Some dissertation writers seem to believe that their task is to get down on the page all they know, and they look to us to tell them what they've said, to shape, cut, and form raw material into an argument. Of course we believe in the power of talking through drafts and trying out ideas, but more and more we value the writer who keeps the eighty-page discovery draft to herself. Or there are writers who give us bare outlines of chapters, filled only with generalities, asking us to see connections and supply evidence. In both cases, we sometimes feel that they expect too much nurture, that we are all too willing (and able) to fix the problem. Rigor becomes not something our students think we expect, but something we'll help them achieve for other, more public (and more important) audiences.

Even given the multiple and conflicting roles we play as we respond to dissertations, we do think the dissertation is important for the way it leads us and our students to new understandings of our teaching and scholarship.

Kate: Let's talk for a minute about what we get out of this mentoring process. I think I learn so much from their work. They always come up with books and angles I've never considered. I also think that maybe there's somebody out there now who is going to move us a little bit closer to a more humane way of doing things. I mean, I'm very interested in sending people out there who will be some sort of agents for change in the system.

Joy: I'm also interested in changing the profession and changing ourselves, and I believe that has to occur through the forms of writing we use. But I also want them to get jobs so they'll be in a position to create change, but I'm hopeful about the experiments and flexibility I see.

Hepsie: I think all of us have an incredible responsibility to try to make the students we send out ethical and human, and it's a tremendous responsibility in a system that is neither ethical nor humane. To the extent that the dissertation is part of that, I think that, just as with my own children, and this gets back to the mother thing, that they can make the world they will have a little better than the world I have.

Kate: But you've always said that if they just believe they're loved, that would be enough.

Hepsie: Your children, yes. Your students, no.

But, it's not always easy to separate our children from our students. Neither the traditional father nor mother roles serves us particularly well. One chapter in Gail Griffin's fine book on feminist teaching *Season of the Witch* (1995) is called "The Space Between: Maternal Pedagogy and the Position of the Woman Teacher." The chapter strongly defends the mother as a model for the teacher by asserting a new definition of mother that makes the role nurturing but not subordinate to a nuclear family father. "We can make a political, historically informed choice to situate ourselves as mothers in explicit contradistinction to the paternal tradition that has shaped academe as we know it. I mean that taking ourselves seriously as maternal pedagogues can give us revolutionary energy" (194). Although we don't want to dismiss our maternal roles, we're still made nervous by Griffin's claim. We turn to different models of the female pedagogue that we believe are less fraught with expectations for unconditional love or support and that offer more fruitful stances for ourselves and our students.

Spinster Love

> Ever since she was just a girl, she was almost certainly told that there was only one way for her to be a full, complete woman. "To be a mother," I said with a nod. "Which she wasn't any good at."
>
> "Or which she may not, deep down, have ever wanted to be," Miss Howard said. ". . . . A man can be a bachelor, and still be a man—because of his mind, his character, his work. But a woman without children? She's a spinster, Stevie—and a spinster is always something less than a woman."
>
> —Caleb Carr (1997), *Angel of Darkness*

If being a spinster means to be "something less than a woman," why would any woman deliberately choose to be one? Part of the answer is that according to the stereotypes of society, which the preceding quote represents, no woman would actually choose to be a spinster. Instead, as countless stories have informed us, the spinster is too unattractive, too asexual, too Puritanical, too plain old mean, to find and hold a man and thus eventually to reap the glories of motherhood that marriage has inevitably occasioned. Her manlessness and her childlessness make her a kind of freak in her community, an object of scorn or pity, marginal as she is to what's been regarded as the real work of women: encouraging men and raising children.

Interestingly enough, the stereotype of the spinster closely matches the caricature of the female teacher. When we sometimes ask our students who are preparing to teach in high schools to characterize the typical English teacher, they always paint the same picture: a dried-up sour-faced bun-wearing old maid. They laugh when they speak of her, knowing the stereotype isn't true—they are planning to be English teachers themselves. Yet it holds power still as their descriptions attest. The teacher is someone who is not a mother, who is not sexual, who may in fact be something less than a woman.

Yet women for centuries have chosen the condition of spinsterhood over motherhood and marriage. The recent recoveries of women's texts from the Middle Ages, many of them written by and about cloistered nuns or religious mystics, show how much agency these women demonstrated in deciding to follow a life path that set them apart from most of their gender. Closer to our own time, women who chose careers in teaching often made a simultaneous choice to remain single. In many school districts across the United States up until the early part of the twentieth century, women who married were forced to leave teaching positions. Among the 1872 rules for teachers posted in the oldest schoolhouse, located in St. Augustine, Florida, number 6 reads, "Women teachers who marry or engage in unseemly conduct will be dismissed" (Salvatori 1996, 142). This rule clearly reflects society's discomfort with women teachers who are also (especially if pregnant) sexual beings. But it also suggests that to be a teacher is to be committed to children who are not one's own, to be not a mother. To be a spinster.

As this history indicates, the spinster teacher was not entirely a revolutionary. The historical accounts above help us see that she, like those around her, was seduced by the religiously sanctioned national narrative of "manifest destiny." She participated in the colonization of the West and implicitly in the exploitation of native peoples and the land. Like Beecher's mothers, she may have enforced the status quo. But, as our own experiences as women in the academy demonstrate, the various roles women play are never simple or singular. Although she may have maintained the status quo in some respects, in other ways the spinster teacher overtly broke from it. She wore no wedding ring, she made her own money, she had her own ideas, and she had no children. In her asexuality, the spinster subverted heterosexual roles and therefore presented more complex possibilities for women.

We found this model helpful in thinking about a story Hepsie told Joy and Kate about a male student who was teaching five sections of composition a semester while he was trying to complete his dissertation. His lack of attention to deadlines, the hurried quality of his drafts, and his lack of preparation for the defense (completed on the very last day before he would lose his graduate student status) made for a difficult, tense, and ultimately unsatisfying experience for him and for her as his advisor. She is critical of the student, who counted too much on her to make everything all right, but more critical of herself for interceding with the committee and the graduate school, for her attempts to scold him into better performances, and for her inability to define their roles as mentor and dissertation writer from the outset: "When one of the members of the committee (and they were all women) pointed out to me that my student would have behaved much differently had I been a man, I realized how big a trap I had fallen into. My colleague was right."

Authority remains an issue not only for females in power but, just as important, for males who answer to them. Stefan had expected Hepsie to nurture him, gently nag him, bail him out, and ultimately see him through. Hepsie concludes that "he would have been surprised, and maybe offended, had I not acted as he expected me to. And his youth, his gender, and his need encouraged me not to disappoint him. For the most part, I behaved just as he expected: like a mom." It would have been useful to escape the trap of motherhood by asserting a new model, not a parent, but a friendly, disinterested supporter. The spinster might have set clearer goals, stated expectations explicitly, and held to them. She might have been loving and generous, but not unconditionally so. She might have helped her graduate student have a more positive, professional experience had she been able to remain more professional herself.

Othermother

> Biological mothers . . . are expected to care for their children. But African and African-American communities have also recognized that vesting one person with full responsibility for mothering a child may not be wise or possible. As a result, othermothers—women who assist bloodmothers by sharing mothering responsibilities—traditionally have been central to the institution of Black motherhood.
>
> —Patricia Hill Collins (1991), *Black Feminist Thought*

The word *spinster* is antiquated and, as we've shown, pejorative in this culture. But the spirit of the spinster—marginal in patriarchal family structure and therefore more independent of it—exists in the African American tradition of the othermother. Patricia Hill Collins' (1991) analysis of the othermother enriches the historical model of the spinster teacher, showing how nontraditional mothers can be vital to the life of the community in nurturing children but also in stimulating intellectual development and a sense of collaborative, communal activism. bell hooks (1989) points out how her own intellectual othermothers created mothering-the-mind relationships that promoted collective inquiry, action, and resistance. We think this version of mothering is useful in further defining alternative roles for women dissertation advisors, roles that might help achieve our goal of changing the way the institution works. We've argued here that one way to change the institution is through writing; the spinster and othermother help us assert that another important way to create change is to alter the institutional structures. As they alter family and community structures, we believe these models can help us reimage our relationships with graduate students and with each other so that we can begin to revise our professional cultures.

In her analysis of black motherhood, Collins (1991) revises the white view of black motherhood perpetuated by politicians, sociologists, ethnographers, and the media who depict them as mammy, matriarch, and welfare mother, or equally damaging and flawed, as "superstrong Black mother," self-sacrificing to a fault, an image Collins says is as "bogus" as the image of the "happy slave" (117). Collins sets out a history of the complex configurations of motherhood arising from West African and Caribbean black societies. One unique role is that of othermothers, who take on mothering roles to other people's children. Othermothers, women who are childless themselves for biological or economic reasons, have a long history, as Collins and Paula Giddings (1984) point out. They are also depicted frequently in writing by African American women, as, for example Frances Ellen Watkins Harper's character Iola Leroy and Alice Walker's Meridian, both of whom become community othermothers.

Collins (1991) argues that the fluid and changing boundaries between biological mothers and other women are directly linked to community activism and values that promote collective rather than individual interests. The othermother, like the spinster, undermines the reverence for the patriarchal, nuclear family with father and mother carrying out their roles of dominance and subservience—a family structure that slavery and economic necessities often made impossible for African Americans. Instead, parenting became a more collaborative, community endeavor; parents did not hold exclusive "rights" over their children, and all members of the community held responsibility for raising children (123). Expanding our maternal roles to encompass the othermother or the spinster can provide us a more useful position from which to advise PhD students. But it is also useful to adapt these models of mentoring because they help us to revise how we think about the intellectual work and the form of the dissertation.

For almost three decades we in composition and rhetoric have asserted the importance of collaborative writing. We claim that collaborative scholarship more authentically approximates the making of knowledge within the discourse communities our students are likely to enter. More important, collaboration challenges monolithic singular conceptions of knowledge and authority. Lisa Ede and Andrea Lunsford (2001) point out the contradictions between our postmodern theoretical stances toward authorship and our professional practices, including the dissertation, which continue to reproduce conventional assumptions about academic work as individual entrepreneurship. Our mentorship of PhD students in the dissertation also still seems to adhere to the nineteenth-century Germanic, paternal model of singular author and authority. This part of our work has remained impervious to collaboration. Of course, our students have committees and readers, but still the one-on-one structure remains in place, because committees and readers often function too peripherally. Joy has experienced the benefits of collaboratively advising PhD students with her colleague Amy Goodburn at a time when Amy was new to the institution. In addition to bringing new faculty more fully into the departmental community, collaborative mentoring benefits students who gain enormously from expertise of other faculty, while they still have the support of someone more experienced in the department and profession. And, as in Joy's experience with Amy, mentors themselves are mentored in these collaborations with colleagues. Most important, discussions about dissertation research between student and multiple collaborative othermothers allow students to experience scholarship as a collaborative intellectual conversation; such discussions support a conception of knowledge as communally, collaboratively constructed rather than as a single-authored monologue.

We acknowledge that the othermother and spinster as versions of dissertation advisor are not without potential problems; faculty must be aware that collaborative advising poses dangers, especially for students. The potential for disagreement and double messages is real, but the conversation required to mediate between different perspectives in the production of the dissertation also more authentically approximates the collaborative development of knowledge that we espouse in theory. It does require that we see a collaborative culture as normal and not threatening to our authority. It demands also that we talk with each other about the responses we're giving to students in order not to derail the students' work, and that we be wary of falling back into good mother/bad father roles.

A more collaborative environment for mentoring graduate students would also encourage each of us to see ourselves—mother, spinster, othermother—as one of a group responsible for students within the larger community, breaking down the patriarchal and potentially oppressive and smothering relationship that we've pointed out and also relieving mentors from the exhausting and isolating mothering relationship. We realize that our PhD students do exist in an extended family, since the three of us function as othermothers among ourselves, listening, advising, commiserating, and cheering each step in the complicated process of seeing a dissertation through to defense, graduation, and the job. Such collaborative structures, if put in place within departments, might help to demystify further the way we work as scholars after the PhD and demonstrate to students how we also function in dialogue and in tension with the departmental and professional cultures.

If much of this essay seems like a complaint, it's also an attempt at self-evaluation, an honest look at the conflicts and struggles we face as we mentor students. Usually, our doctoral students don't know about those struggles, nor do they know about the problems we have as writers or as teachers that may complicate our work with them. We've not let them in. Looking back, we realize that we have far too often, despite our collaborative intention and antipatriarchal belief, held on to a wise old seer persona that prevents us from sharing our own difficulties and that discourages our students from taking more authority themselves. Our reflection here, we hope, is a step toward reconceiving the woman dissertation director's role as less monolithic and more multiple—sometimes a spinster, sometimes a mother, sometimes the othermother. At the very least we hope that naming and investigating these multiple roles will help all of us—who simultaneously act as students and mentors—remain agitated as we go about the work of nurturing the intellect.

Chapter Seven

"She Herself Is the Writing," But the Form Doesn't Fit

The Dissertation as a Site of Becoming

Cindy Moore and Peggy Woods

As graduate students from two different institutions about to begin their dissertations, Cindy Moore and Peggy Woods met during the 1995 Conference on College Composition and Communication at a roundtable on the dissertation. Intrigued by the intersections of their work, they continued their conversation via email in a manner that looked something like this.

Dear Peggy:

I like your idea about putting on paper the concerns we shared during our session on dissertation writing.

I remember how fascinated, but also worried, I was when, as a new PhD student, I listened to an ABD in our program describe the sense of psychic split she had experienced throughout dissertation writing. Her director wanted a dissertation written from a distanced, detached perspective. Yet because the research informing her dissertation was naturalistic, interpretive, my friend wanted a dissertation whose voice was more personal, more "true" to the spirit of her project, to her own spirit as a scholar. Unable to establish common ground with her director, she ended up writing two dissertations: one for her director and one for herself. It is the latter version that she returns to with enthusiasm, that gives her a sense of accomplishment and pride. It is the latter version that she plans to shape into a book manuscript because, as she says, "No one will want to read the other one anyway."

At the time, I was steeped in feminist critical theory. I couldn't help noticing how my friend's schizophrenic feelings were shared by critics like Jane Tompkins, Marianna Torgovnick, Nancy Mairs, and Rachel Blau DuPlessis—women who were trying to express their feelings about literature in a form that forced them to speak in voices, to take on identities, that felt foreign to them, painfully alien. And both of us commented on the seeming disjunction between the calls for broader conceptions of acceptable voices in composition and rhetoric and the reality of dissertation writing.

Certainly no two dissertations are identical, but at the U of Louisville they seem to share a set of characteristics: an objective, distanced rhetorical stance; a linear structure; a privileging of "evidence" over intuition or personal experience. As I mentioned in April, I'm having trouble imagining how findings from my dissertation study will fit into the conventional form. I'm planning an ethnographic study of an advanced writing class called "Feminist Expository Writing." Class participants will be reading feminist theories of language, voice, and subjectivity and experimenting with "feminist" forms of exposition and argument—forms that are multivocal, nonlinear, personal. In keeping with the feminist design of the course, I'm planning to use feminist research methods that emphasize collaboration with participants and researcher-reflection. The question that's been eating at me is this: How can I maintain the personal, reflective essence of my project if I write a typical dissertation, using the traditional academic voice and style? On the other hand, if I break with convention, will my work appear less scholarly, less rigorous? Will *I* appear unqualified for an academic position? Anxious to hear your thoughts on all of this. . . . Cindy

Dear Cindy,

When we first met, I was beginning to wrestle with how to reconcile my seemingly diverse interests in feminist theory, narrative theory, and composition theory. I saw myself as a fiction writer whose interests were in how the boundaries between these various discourses are and could be blurred. I was beginning to question how a dissertation could be written in order to reflect these interests as well as reflect the kind of writer I am. Since our panel, I have imagined many different forms or shapes my dissertation could take. I am fortunate that in my department we are encouraged to push at the boundaries and write nontraditional dissertations. So as you might guess, there are many alternative dissertation models available to me. Some of the models I considered were writing a series of short stories that attempt to enact and embody various feminist strategies; writing primarily in academic prose and speaking directly to the influences, differences, and similarities between fiction writing, feminist narrative theory, and composition theory; dividing my dissertation into sections—the first half discussing the theory, the second half consisting of the fiction that enacts the theories; writing a critical essay for each short story that makes visible the theories that had informed the writing of the stories.

Although I certainly have the support of my committee, I still feel I must ask myself why I do not want to fall into the trap I have seen students and fellow workshop members fall into—they write clever, wild, far-out stuff because they can. And although I have the freedom to write any of these dissertations, what is the purpose of doing so? Should I write a nontraditional dissertation just because I can? What do I hope to accomplish? What do I really want to do? Are the dissertations that I imagine an accurate representation of who I imagine myself to be, the kind of writer/scholar I wish to be seen as?

Please don't get me wrong—I am glad that I have all these choices available to me. However, in spite of the range of options and the encouragement I receive here, I still feel constrained by the consequences of writing such a dissertation. My work still needs to be read outside of our particular graduate program, by people who may not be as sympathetic. This is, of course, a concern of my committee as well.

Now that I have gone through the exam and prospectus, it has become apparent that underlying all my other interests has been the question of form. How does form relate to content? How intertwined are they? Should the form mirror the content? Is it always effective to do so?

Do you remember John Barth's story "Lost in the Funhouse"? How while the narrator is telling us the story he throws in various rules of narrative and then immediately breaks them? At first it seems too confusing to read; the constant interruptions seem too distracting and your first impulse as a reader is to try to ignore the interruptions. However, as you go through the story you begin to realize this isn't really just a story about a family going to Atlantic City. This is a story about narrative, writers, and the kinds of choices writers make as they construct stories. Barth could have written this piece in many different ways in order to call attention to the diverse ways in which narratives are constructed. However, Barth's decision to combine the theory with the fiction moves this discussion to a different level. By allowing the choices, the rules, and the conventions that inform every story to break through the surface, Barth enables and actually forces the reader to see how constructed narratives are.

And this is what I want to do. In my dissertation I want to show the relationship between fiction and theory, how theory and fiction are intertwined, how the theory informs my fiction. The question before me then seems to be what form will best do this?

Peggy:

Yes, the pressures to conform (even in a program like yours) seem substantial. As you say, even if your professors embrace innovation, it appears that academia, in general, doesn't—at least where students, the not-yet-fully-initiated, are concerned. But scholars like David Kaufer and Cheryl Geisler argue that writers are unable to think like "insiders" when they are discouraged from taking risks in their writing. Real community members (real writers, real scholars) succeed, after all, because of their ability to take what others have done further, to think new thoughts, create new boundaries, landscapes. I'm wondering how we (as dissertation writers, as women poised for professorial positions) can possibly market ourselves as academic insiders if we don't write, "speak" like insiders in the very work that will certify us for those positions.

And then there's the matter of theory. Theories about writing and writers are constantly changing, and, as Barth demonstrates, such change must somehow be reflected in (or accommodated by) our texts. Otherwise, it's just "art for art's sake"—something static, divorced from the creator, the creative context. DuPlessis uses many of the same strategies as Barth throughout *The Pink Guitar*. In "For the Etruscans," her essay on the status of women writers and women's writing, DuPlessis suggests that linear, univocal, traditional textual forms simply can't accommodate the multiplicity, the fluidity of women's lives. Like Barth, she takes things to a different (and I would argue more interesting) level in her collage-type essays, which mingle "academic" and "personal" perspectives, which blur the boundaries between poetry and prose. Yet, for DuPlessis, it's not just about mirroring current theories in the texts we write; it's about bringing our writing lives and our other lives (as friends, parents, partners, daughters) together in a manner that celebrates this variety, fullness.

If I look around at what's going on in composition and rhetoric these days, I see the same kind of effort to develop structures and styles that incorporate various writing voices, subjectivities, selves: McCarthy and Fishman's "Boundary Conversations," Connors and Lunsford's "Ma & Pa Kettle Do Research," and more recently, Kathleen Dixon's "Gendering the Personal." All of these writers stretch conventional discursive boundaries and, in so doing, allow for new versions, new visions of "theorist," "academic," "researcher." As a dissertation writer interested in these developments, I can't help wondering where (and if) I'll be able to enter this current conversation. With what voice, what self, will I be able to speak?

On that note, I leave you for today. I must go and buy a new computer monitor.

Best. . . . Cindy

Dear Cindy,

Once again it appears we are living parallel lives. You are off to buy a computer monitor and I must pack mine off to the repair shop. It seems everything I own is beginning to wear out—my car, my computer, my clothes. Sometimes I think the real motivating force behind finishing my dissertation is economic.

After reading your last note I was reminded of Michelle Cliff's "Journey into Speech" and how after she wrote her dissertation she was not sure who she had become. Cliff says that although her dissertation was responsible for giving her an intellectual belief in herself that she had not had before, it at the same time distanced her from and rendered her *speechless* about who she was. It seems standing here at the beginning of the dissertation process, we feel similar to Cliff. Conventional academic writing allows us, enables us to feel "smart," to feel "intelligent." Our ability to produce carefully constructed academic prose signifies we are a part of the academic community. Our finished dissertations will be visible proof that we belong. But is this who we really are? Who we really want to be?

Cliff also discusses what she calls a "history of forced fluency." The academic essay she (and we have) learned to master, is rooted in a logical construction. This construction enables us to adopt a particular subject position (dominant, authoritative) and voice (smart). We are beginning to question this subject position, this voice. Why is this particular voice the privileged voice? What does this particular voice prevent us from saying? From knowing?

Have you had a chance to look through Jeanette Winterson's *Art [Objects]*? In the title essay, Winterson defines the "true/real/gifted" writer as someone who only sounds like him or herself. To sound like another writer is an imitation. Of course I don't completely agree with this because I am not sure how unique anyone can really be, and I also think tradition has established a range of how different anyone can really sound. I do think, though, writers (creative *and* academic) not only experience finding their own voices; they understand voice and the construction of voice as a choice they make. For some, this is not only a question of form, but of merger, of reconciling these two voices.

Peggy:

Sorry it's taken me so long to reply. I've been in the midst of my study and also just had my baby! (We named him Bill.) As you can imagine, things are hectic.

I've been thinking a lot about that authority issue, too. I agree that we need to think more about the "voice of authority"—especially in terms of the selves it presumes to speak, who it excludes. It seems that if the "voice of authority" is a singular, unified thing, then we abandon the whole idea of rhetorical context (audience, purpose, etc.) or narrow possible contexts significantly. With respect to the dissertations I've skimmed in my department, the audience seems limited to committee members, the purpose to getting the degree. I want to imagine a bigger audience, a larger purpose for my work. I mean, aren't I supposed to try to get this stuff published fairly quickly after I graduate?

I have more to write, but I need to get home. (Unfortunately, I don't have a modem there.)

I'm back . . .

To continue . . . I think what we're saying is that the dissertation process is an identity-shaping activity. Through it, we're supposed to come into our professional self. But we don't see this as a unified position, with discernible boundaries and a common voice; we see it as multiple, fluid, a collection of many selves.

The conformity thing . . . sometimes, I think it's a result of people not seeing themselves as writers *at all*. If you don't see yourself as a writer, creator, then it's hard to imagine the importance of what we're saying. Seems like we see ourselves as writers first and as academics or scholars second.

A related issue concerns genre boundaries. People still have a hard time accepting that elements of traditional expository prose can be profitably mingled with elements of poetry and fiction. (Again, I want to say something like "Real writers write that way!") In the class I've been observing, students have a hard time believing it's okay, legitimate, to bridge academic and creative genres, because, of course, it's not okay according to our course schedules (which separate creative writing from composition) and according to most of their professors.

Thankfully, my director accepts the idea that, because I'll be writing about a class whose very purpose is to exploit these boundaries, the form of my dissertation should challenge accepted conventions. Yet, she still gets nervous when I talk about "big" structural breaks—like including my methods section as an appendix. ("Your readers will have certain expectations.") And then there's the rest of my committee. They want to be open to change, but, at the same time, they worry. . . . Cindy

Dear Cindy,

Congratulations!! That is great news about the baby. I hope everyone is doing well.

Once again your last note reminds me of Winterson's essay "Art Objects." In this piece she defines the true artist as someone who is connected to the past and who makes a connection to the future. It seems this is a position we also occupy. Our dissertations are supposed to come out of a set of traditions, but are also supposed to further the collective body of knowledge within the field of English. It seems our entrance into the profession is based not only on our resemblance to those who have come before us, but also on our potential for making meaningful contributions to the future. We must somehow reconcile traditions in order to stay connected to our scholarly pasts, but we also must be innovative in order to make a connection to the future.

My own dissertation is very much like this. I have created a narrator who, as a woman writer, struggles to reconcile all her various pasts in order to create her own poetics. She attempts not only to reconcile her own personal pasts with the literary tradition she sees herself writing out of, but also to reconcile all the literary histories she identifies with as a late twentieth-century woman writer—the conventional and familiar literary history beginning with Defoe, as well as the feminist tradition beginning with Austen. Although my narrator feels she is more a part of the feminist tradition than the more familiar line, she realizes that she cannot simply throw away all that she has learned, all that has influenced her in some way.

I think we are in a position similar to my narrator. It seems that along with attempting to reconcile our pasts, we are also attempting to reconcile all the various voices we speak with (and out of). Like DuPlessis, we desire not only to reconcile, but to give space to the personal voices we have. We are also trying to reconcile familiar dissertation conventions not just with various theories, but with other forms of scholarship. This, I think, is also our contribution.

I think the challenge facing us is more complex than simply deciding either to copy and stay within the norm or to be innovative. I think all writers face the problem of deciding how innovative to be. It seems if we are too innovative we run the risk of being dismissed. In our specific cases if our dissertations are *too* creative, *too* far out there, break *too* much with the accepted conventions, we run the risk of being denied entrance into the academic community that will allow us to continue our work.

It seems a balance needs to be struck between imitation and innovation. But when does too much innovation prevent us from even being heard? I think what I am asking is how much of the conventions and traditions do we need and want to preserve?

P—

Yeah, part of the problem may be the fear of someone taking things too far. Sometimes, when I tell people I'd like to write my dissertation in a feminist form (which I define as having both academic and personal or creative elements), I get the sense that they are imagining something indecipherable. In "Me and My Shadow" (do you know that piece?), Jane Tompkins talks about the conflict between feeling she must break with "masculine" tradition and knowing that, if she does, she risks "not being heard." Many feminists would point out that it's not an either/or proposition. That is, we don't write either the "same ol' same ol'" or something wholly unfamiliar, but instead we write something that combines elements of both. We communicate with readers using some of the structures and signposts they're used to seeing, while at the same time introducing textual innovations. Such a synthesis is very difficult to achieve; it's much easier to write either the conventional academic, thesis-driven article or a free-verse poem. And I don't think genre-crossing works for every subject, every audience. Seems that analysis of rhetorical context becomes especially important when we attempt something new. Maybe we need to more effectively communicate our sense of audience to our committees? Maybe they just don't realize that we have clear purposes in mind? And maybe they don't see that our articulations of audience and purpose can guide them in their assessment of our projects?

Another fear is that our innovations will be viewed by prospective employers as unprofessional. (I have been thinking about that one a lot lately.) Again, though, is this concern really valid? If there is risk associated with innovation, how great is the risk? What is really at stake if we express the various aspects of ourselves in our dissertations? (Seems we know what's at stake if we don't: our emotional and mental well being—and, I would argue, the sanity of our friends and families. Maybe even the health of the profession as a whole.)

Perhaps, too, professors who worry about student innovation have too much invested in the status quo to be interested in change. After all, implied in our desire to do something different is a criticism of the writing they did to enter their fields, to get tenure, recognition. If their identities are mingled with their writing styles—H.D. (1961) says, after all, that "we are the writing"—then it's as if we're attacking who they are by questioning how they write. While I don't wish to criticize any single person, I'm afraid that if I don't challenge tradition, my dissertation will end up being just another hoop to jump through—something that doesn't hold any real meaning for me now or in the future.

Later. . . . Cindy

P.S. I forgot to ask—are you on the job market this year?

Dear Cindy,

I know, like me, you must be completely buried under with teaching, working on your dissertation, and more recently, all the job market stuff (yes, I'm on the market this year) and unlike me, running after the baby. I wanted to tell you about what happened in my class yesterday that got me thinking about our ongoing conversation about identity and voice.

In the critical writing class I am currently teaching, I asked the students to read Adrienne Rich's essay, "When We Dead Awaken"—you know, the one in which Rich talks about re-vision as "the act of looking back at something with fresh eyes, entering an old text from a new critical direction." I had the students read this essay and then try to re-vision their own revision process. I put them in groups to do this and as usual there was one group off-task. Rather than talking about re-vision, this group of three women was discussing how their identities had changed or would change after marriage—two of the women in this group were already married. Listening to what they had to say, I began to realize that they were discussing a re-visioning of their own identities. Later during our class discussion, I began to think about writers, the identities different writers have or we believe they have, and how sometimes we need to re-vision who writers are.

It seems that as dissertation writers, we are involved in this process of re-visioning—not only re-visioning who we are, but re-visioning our own voices. I see myself currently in this re-vision stage, moving from grad student to a professional in English studies. I am not only attempting to re-vision who I am, to re-vision the identities I need and want to assume, but I am also attempting to sort out which voice(s) to speak with.

By identifying myself as a writer first and a scholar second it may seem I am saying I am searching for my own voice rather than trying to adopt a voice that will guarantee me entrance into the academy. When we write creatively, we adopt a particular kind of voice, when we write as scholars we adopt another particular kind of voice. Yet I think what interests us both are the possibilities that occur when the two are merged—or the space where both of the voices merge out of. That is, I wonder if we could take things even a bit further and say the dissertation itself is not only an act of re-vision, but a process of reconciliation. As we work to re-vision our selves and our voices, it seems we are also simultaneously engaged in the process of reconciling all the identities we have and had as well as all the voices we speak with.

Due to my personal reasons for entering graduate school, I never really thought of my dissertation as my last school assignment or my entrance into the academic community. I saw it as my chance to write, the creation of the space that authorized work on a project I wanted to work on. Although I enjoy writing and working on my project, the pressures I feel this year (academically and economically) are forcing me to re-vision my dissertation. Every semester I spend writing my dissertation not only puts me deeper into debt, but delays my entrance into the job market. The temptation to write a conventional dissertation is great because it seems like the easiest thing to do and once I graduate and have a tenure-track job, I can really write what I want. But *is* it the easiest or the best thing to do? *Does* having a tenure-track position guarantee the time and the freedom to work on the project I really want to write?

Well these are just some thoughts I wanted to throw out. I hope all is going well. How is the job search going? Any news? Are you going to CCCC in March? I'll be there, and hopefully we will be able to hook up for coffee or something. Talk to you soon. —Peggy

Dear Peggy:

Are you still out there? Great news! I was offered, and accepted, a position at IU-PU, Fort Wayne. I really like the people, and the location seems similar to where I'm from. Anyway, I'm glad the whole job-search process is over.

One aspect of the application/interviewing process that interests me is how one must consciously think through who one wants to be (or appear to be)

in letters, when talking with people. Maybe you experienced this, too—the strange sense of describing yourself as you are describing your dissertation and maybe emphasizing one aspect of yourself over another in certain situations? I remember thinking, "Oh, I better not stress the feminist aspect of this too much at that school," or "Probably I should downplay the personal voice of my dissertation." Finally, though, I remembered why I wanted to write a feminist, innovative dissertation in the first place—so I could express a multiple, rich, "real" variety of selves. So I took the job where the people seemed to appreciate that variety, where I would not be expected to be either an academic or a writer, a professional or a mother, woman, friend, etc. It all seems to go together.

Remember how we were talking about the way the form or style of our writing helps shape our identities? Well now, after writing half of my dissertation, I understand how the form can determine what we see in terms of content, too. Initially I had conceived my second chapter as the first part of a long narrative about the class I observed. I was going to write it as the beginning of a story, focusing on the students' responses to the first assignment that asked them to develop a new form of academic writing. As I started the very linear account, I realized that it wasn't capturing the essence of the class—particularly the sense of innovation and risk that I observed as students tried to mingle poetry and prose, incorporate multiple voices, play with words, with extended metaphors. I decided to try a collage-type design (after DuPlessis' "For the Etruscans") where I went back and forth between three primary narratives. What I found is that by juxtaposing the pieces of one narrative against the pieces of another, I discovered ideas, interpretations that I simply would not have been able to see if I had written a single, uninterrupted narrative. I could also feel the difficulty many of the students experienced as they tried to extend the borders of acceptable academic writing. Piecing together the narratives and then mingling them in a way that would make sense to a traditionally trained reader was difficult and time-consuming. As the clock ticked me closer to my spring deadline, I kept wondering if it might have been better just to do something more normal. Yet, the adventure of seeing new things through formal innovation kept me believing that, in the long run, the time and anxiety would be worth it. And I think it will. Or I keep telling myself that! How about you?

Dear Cindy,

IPFW! No way! I just had a phone interview with them about a visiting creative writing position! Wouldn't that be funny if we both ended up there? Congratulations on the job, too. It is great to see that this whole process actually works!

We have talked so much before about how to situate ourselves, how to represent ourselves in the academy in terms of our dissertation. However, I have found, like you, the job search adds another layer to my thinking on voice and identity. After being on the market these past few months and writing the cover letters and the dissertation abstract, and discussing my dissertation with interviewers, I have discovered it isn't so much our dissertations that define who we are, but rather how we represent our dissertations. As I struggled to boil my 300-plus page dissertation into a one-page abstract and into one paragraph of my cover letter, I came to realize that what I said about my dissertation was the closest many people would ever come to reading it. I don't mean this to be cynical, but I realized that if I was unable to convey in one paragraph the depth, the connections, the levels and kinds of intersections my dissertation makes, my application would never reach the second-look pile. It seems that although we are done with our dissertations, we still have one more step to go. How do we represent the work we have done? My committee wanted to be sure that my application wouldn't be dismissed because I had written a creative dissertation. So although I said I wrote a fictional *and* critical dissertation (or critical *and* fictional depending on how I wanted to be seen), does this still accurately represent my work in a way that would enable a search committee to imagine someone like me, whose writing and research interests are not so readily and easily categorized, being in their department?

Dear Cindy,

I don't know if you have heard the good news yet, but I was offered and accepted the creative writing position at IPFW! So it looks like we will be colleagues! It will be great to be able to have face-to-face conversations in addition to our cybertalks. (Hey, how is your dissertation coming along? Did you defend yet?)

Well now that the semester, the job search, and graduation (Yeah!) are over it seems I can begin to reflect on this entire dissertation process. This summer I am going to teach a course called "Writing a Woman's Life," and as I have been preparing for this class it has occurred to me that my dissertation is in a sense just that—the writing of a woman's life, a woman who develops and constructs her own poetics in order to claim her own authority as a writer. What seems rather strange to me now that the dissertation is completed is that although my narrator is able to assert herself as a writer, I am left still wondering what kind of a writer and scholar am I? How does this dissertation situate me within the academy?

Throughout the majority of the writing process I felt my dissertation was basically a novel. There is really only one "real" academic-type essay within it. The rest of the pieces are cross-genre, short stories, and one entire novella. All of this is held together by a first-person narrator who finds many of the pieces to read and then writes the novella throughout the text. However, after reading the entire dissertation, my committee felt I had written a book on narrative theory. How did this happen?

Although I was puzzled at first by their response, once I actually read the entire text from beginning to end I agreed with them—this was not a novel. So my question is again—how did this happen? How can something that is written using narrative conventions and forms be read and seen as theory? Maybe this isn't a question for this particular conversation, but a question dealing with the intersections of academic and creative writing. Maybe the question is more a question of voice. Did I, like Michelle Cliff, lose my "fiction" voice? Did being in the academy, going through the whole process of graduate school, somehow not only develop my scholarly voice, but merge, intertwine it with my narrative voice? Was the writing of my dissertation a way for me to discover who I had now become, rather than a conscious effort to declare who I thought I was? Hmmmmm—I'll end here. —Peggy

Hi Peggy,

About my dissertation: I will be defending June 8th. I'm not sure what to expect. I imagine part of the defending will involve explaining why I wrote the dissertation the way I did. For that fact—and for many other reasons—I'm glad we've kept up this correspondence.

Like you, I experienced a shifting of identities as I wrote my dissertation in different styles. I used a narrative frame for the overall story of the class and spoke mostly in present tense, as if I was writing the dissertation as I was observing. Every once in a while I would interrupt the narrative to analyze the observations—thus taking on a more "objective," scholarly like identity—or to insert more personal thoughts, reflections. I felt myself assuming the identity of "poet" each time I did something innovative with structure or style. (The collage design of the second chapter felt poetic to me, as did parts where I actually wrote in lyrical lines, rhythms.) In Chapter Four I included a narrative of one student within the larger class narrative. I wrote this inner narrative in letter form, using a more colloquial language and a different font. And in my last chapter, I tried to recreate my own struggles with perfectionism by juxtaposing, in dialogic form, the voice of the "good girl writing" against the voice of the innovative dissertation writer. I guess what I'm getting at is that I was finding my way through different positions, different selves as I wrote—something that would not have been possible had I written the "standard dissertation." And, as I mentioned before, I found that I needed to move into different positions, take on different identities, to see different angles on my subject matter. I could see one angle from the storyteller point of view, another angle from the scholar-researcher point of view, another from the student point of view. Ideally, all of these points of view could coexist in one style. But, at present, I'm finding the tension among styles, among identities, useful somehow, as if the gaps hold secrets, surprises.

In the class I studied, I saw the same movement between identities at work among students. Many of the students were English majors—juniors and seniors who were adept at minding their discursive manners. Part of their identities as good students was mingled with their ability to write standard academic prose. So when they moved away from that, they seemed to experience shifts away from their student identities. Some of those who wrote on explicitly feminist topics shifted into positions of "woman" or "activist"—positions not allowed for by their usual classroom writing.

So, I think, again, "We are the writing."

I think, too, it's promising that more people are being encouraged to take on more than one identity in academia. You were encouraged to combine a fiction-writer identity with that of "scholar." My encouragement hasn't been as direct as yours, but I have felt my attempts at combining a more scholarly identity with a more creative one affirmed finally by my readers—or, at least, not rejected. What helped me, I gather, was that my director and committee members knew I could write the traditional way; I had done so in their classes. (The ol' know-the-rules-before-you-can-break-them thing.)

Back to my defense. I imagine someone pointing out how narrative makes the research seem constructed, that is, not objective enough. My own feeling is that narrative calls attention to the constructedness that's there anyway. We're always telling a story, whether we do it explicitly, through narrative, or less obviously, through plain speech, objective argument. And, sometimes the least apparently constructed writing is, in truth, the most constructed.

Did you find an apartment yet? Let me know when you get to Fort Wayne. It will be nice to be in the same city, to talk about these issues in closer proximity.

Although several years have passed and Cindy and Peggy once again find themselves at different institutions—Cindy now in Minnesota and Peggy in Massachusetts—their discussion continues. As they draft conference papers and articles, and compile annual review files, they continue to wonder how best to integrate their various interests and identities, how best to reconcile past voices with future desires.

Chapter Eight

Writing Wrong: The Dissertation as Dissent

Devan Cook and Darrell Fike

Completing a dissertation signifies the candidate's seriousness as he or she bids for entry into the academy; the text itself exists both as evidence that the initiation process is complete and as a guide along the route into teaching, publishing, and tenure. But we rarely think of the dissertation as a pedagogical site wherein the candidate's bid for credentials becomes intertwined with class, gender, and disciplinary politics within the academy. "Why do the major academic pedagogies continue to reflect . . . an individual, solitary, masculine knower," Andrea Lunsford (1992) has asked of the classroom, ". . . bringing that individual into assimilation with some economic, cultural, or psychological status quo?" (66). Nowhere is this fictional "knower" constructed more obviously than in the "classroom" of the traditional dissertation, with its authoritative, soliloquizing, "objective" voice that reifies academic power structures.

Looking back, this is easy to see. But as recent graduates of a doctoral program that accepts both critical and creative dissertations, we were surprised at the difficulties we experienced in completing dissertations that did not neatly fit into either category and instead attempted to interrogate the boundaries of both. In one case, a creative dissertation that began as a poetry collection evolved to include a hypertext-style layer of critical commentary informed by contemporary literary and rhetorical theory. In the other case, an ethnographic study investigating the writing lives of working students grew to include a parallel autobiographical text examining the author's history as a working student in writing classes. But even as our projects were growing, evolving, and seeking to shape the profession we were entering and the scholars we would be within the profession, multiple forces were at work to shape and limit our nontraditional projects and fix them within traditional, recognized boundaries.

Perhaps our experiences would have been less disconcerting had we examined more closely the rhetorical situation of the nontraditional dissertation—its locus and context—and been prepared for the resistance and anxiety we encountered, to which the following stories bear evidence. Never did we stop to consider English department hierarchies, which privilege literature and criticism over creative writing and composition; never did we consider that to some the boundaries between these subdisciplines of English studies, which we transgressed with gleeful impunity, look like international borders. Despite our critical training and interest, we thought little about gender or class and work history and how they related to the dissertation, a credentialing document in a discipline-specific genre.

Middle-aged and worldly though we are, we were naïve. Here we share the histories of our dissertations in order to explain the shapes and contexts of our problems. Through these histories we'll consider how the academy, through the dissertation process, seeks to shape doctoral candidates into Lunsford's "solitary, individual, masculine knower" while candidates, dissenting from and playing with established disciplinary boundaries, attempt to fracture the monolith of academic discourse and power.

Where Qualitative Research, Memoir, and Composition Meet

Devan Cook

Writing a nontraditional dissertation is challenging for a candidate and potentially disruptive to the credentialing system. Given composition's ambiguous or marginalized position vis-à-vis the established hierarchy in many English departments (Miller 1991; Scholes 1985), this situation is problematic indeed. In this regard Florida State University, where Darrell and I both studied, is typical. Ultimately, issues of and questions about authority—the authority of the academic persona created by the dissertation writer and the authority of the postsecondary apparatus that grants its imprimatur to that writer—are raised by the form of the nontraditional dissertation. In composition, some play seems to be allowed. But how much? And where? And whose?

It's easy to forget how hard I worked trying to construct an academic persona who would sound as though she had sufficient authority to receive the PhD. That I was attempting to write a nontraditional dissertation in which I consciously blurred disciplinary and genre boundaries between anthropology, composition, and creative nonfiction made the problem of constructing such a persona more difficult. Without a traditional field or a set of accepted discursive practices to refer to, establishing authority is difficult no matter how supportive and intelligent readers are and how skilled the author may be in mapping out the rhetorical situation of the text. I had problems with addressing the evaluative expectations of readers, with establishing my own authority in the academy, with understanding what was required. Often, too, my problems were related to my status as a woman doctoral candidate in love with her project (Aisenberg and Harrington 1988).

My dissertation, "Literacies at Work: The Writing Lives of Working Students," was based on case studies of twenty-three such students; it also dealt with the process of researching the case studies. Given the phenomenological nature of ethnographic inquiry and the way it relies on the researcher's ideas, attitudes, behaviors, contexts, histories, and language as its primary research instruments (Denzin and Lincoln 1994; Punch 1986), I was never able to separate myself as researcher from those whose lives I researched. What I learned was as messy, rough, and haphazard as the writing lives of working students often are: one *non sequitur* after another. The rhetorical situations of their lives paralleled in many ways the rhetorical situation of writing my dissertation, and I wanted my dissertation itself to reflect that.

Producing a conventionally ordered work about unconventional and disorderly writing lives seemed distasteful to me, a choice replicating once again the hierarchies and exclusions that permeate working students' experiences. But I still faced the need to make some choices about order and focus. Was the dissertation, the whole research and writing process, about the writing lives of working students (and about me, since for many years I was one); about a research guide, a sort of Hitchhiker's Guide to the Galaxy of ethnographic writing research; or about the recursive, ambiguous, local, frustrating, and often humorous nature of ethnography itself? In order to write the dissertation, I would have to decide.

I could have looked at my field notes, research logs, and interview transcripts, reviewed the literature, and drawn some conclusions. Viewed that way, my enterprise sounds rather cut-and-dried. But simply figuring out what the dissertation was supposed to look like, what sort of form it might conceivably take, was difficult. As Keith Fort (1971) writes, "The first question always asked about a prospective paper is whether the idea is 'workable' or can be 'handled.' As I understand these terms, they mean 'do you have a thesis that can be proved?' This formal requirement is a *sine qua non* for a paper" (631).

While I could draw few conclusions from my field research (one I finally produced was that working students have such full lives, it's surprising they get any writing done) and thus wasn't in a good position to present my findings in a conventional format, I had something to say: about the untapped, largely unknown contexts within which our students write, with untapped, unknown consequences; about the experience, character, and wisdom of the research participants; about qualitative methodologies in writing research; about the value in finding myself as I neared my personal ivory tower's pinnacle, so much a lost and confused student; about research and writing as spiritual locations and practices; about—humility, about going through the process of becoming an expert to find I wasn't one.

In writing three complete drafts of my dissertation, I tried several strategies, using as models two books—Peter Elbow's *What Is English?* and Margery Wolf's *A Thrice-Told Tale. What Is English?* alternates between traditional commentary and interview transcripts or journal selections from other teachers, which break up the text, share authority, and represent English as a broad and various field indeed. In *A Thrice-Told Tale* Margery Wolf uses three genres—field notes, short story, and journal article—to present the field research she conducted in China. I found it a wonderfully effective book, capturing as nothing else I'd read the incredible variety and complexity of what can be learned by doing ethnography. This was, of course, exactly what I wanted my dissertation to achieve.

So with great naïveté, I conflated the rhetorical situation of established professionals with my own. For my first draft, I wrote a series of related essays interspersed with excerpts from research logs, interview transcripts, poems, and personal memoir pieces. Coherence—or rather, its lack—was an issue: My director suggested that I try to show a reader how to read the piece while keeping some of the flavor, immediacy, and metawriting that the collage afforded.

"Put most of this primary evidence [interviews, transcripts, researcher's perspective] in appendices," she said. I did so in the second draft, stripping the text, outlining, imposing order. In fact, the order began to dictate the writing: I selected for what I wanted to say, not for what actually happened. But ethnographic research is not about control, and the draft was misleading. It was easier to read, but also less honest, believable, and authoritative. I returned to my director.

"When I suggest extensive revisions, why don't you get upset?" she wanted to know. I couldn't understand why I might be bothered—I wanted a dissertation I could defend successfully yet one that honored my reasons for writing. And I wanted it written before I ran out of money. She was helping me to achieve this. Why should I be angry or hurt?

"Put back transcript selections for reliability," she said. We discussed how I might derail somewhat the imperative of point-making: In the third draft, I added a chapter discussing students who didn't fit, who disproved my thesis. I also regularized the chapter formatting. The text was easier to deal with but was faithful to the research experience.

All of the poems were in appendices. "My goodness," said another committee member. "When I got to the end, there was all this great stuff. I wish I had known sooner that it was there."

As a dissertation writer I had, with the help of a supportive director and committee, constructed an authoritative academic persona, and the dissertation was accepted. But I still question that persona. In the rhetorical situation of my dissertation, there are not one but two speakers. One is primary, foregrounded, official, and credentialed—she's "Dr. Cook." The other, filled with personal knowledge and passionate convictions, whispers.

Discovering Who Is Speaking: The Story of My Dissertation

Darrell Fike

> First question: who is speaking?
> Who, among the totality of speaking individuals, is
> accorded the right to use this sort of language?
> —M. Foucault (1972), *The Archaeology of Knowledge*

Admitted to Florida State University as a writing program student, I knew that I would have the option of writing either a scholarly or a creative dissertation.

The prospect of spending four or five years immersed in a study of poetry that would culminate in producing my own collection was irresistibly alluring. Reading and writing poetry with others who agonized over stanza lengths or line breaks appealed deeply to my love of words. A commitment to a creative dissertation would mean a commitment to living my life as a poet, as someone who proclaimed poetry as a priority in life, not just a few scribbles hidden away in a journal book. With a doctorate and a collection of poems, I would emerge from graduate school as a professor and a poet, eager to share my love of language through teaching and writing.

After learning a bit more about the ways and means of the academy, however, I began to have doubts about pursuing a purely creative dissertation. Despite hearing of a few job search successes from other creative writing graduates, I sensed that many in the greater academic world are not convinced creative-dissertation writers are legitimate scholars. While coursework, qualifying exams, published journal articles, and professional presentations might suggest that a creative dissertator has been through a rigorous enough curriculum to meet the demands of most teaching assignments, the lack of a scholarly dissertation seems to raise a suspicious eyebrow or two on hiring committees. Recognizing the importance of the dissertation in terms of the job market and professional identity, I worried that I would be less employable if I completed a creative dissertation.

So while my heart told me to pursue my lifelong interest in poetry, my head and my wallet urged me to swallow hard and write a traditional scholarly dissertation—no matter how arcane or boring it might be—that might lead more quickly to full-time employment in the academy, along with the enticing promise of medical insurance, a pension, and professional acceptance.

Dutifully, I cast about for a traditional course of study that would allow me to study poetry but result in a dissertation that would be recognized as an effort worthy of a doctoral candidate in English. For a while I thought I would write a dissertation on some aspect of poetic theory or critically examine a poet's work. I checked out a few literature professors and began to think of topics that might serve as a vehicle to help me improve my own poetry and result in a traditional scholarly dissertation.

But here is where I came to a dead-end: I never really had a feel for what that scholarly dissertation might be. My intellectual interests and my passion were wedded to writing my own poetry. So for two years, I floundered around, wondering just what in the hell I was doing with my life. Finally, I committed to a creative dissertation and allied myself with My First Major Professor, an established poet in the department. I took workshops, attended readings, and wrote poem after poem, but still I worried about my dissertation's status and about my own intellectual development. I still felt somewhat uncertain and adrift, despite my commitment to this professor and a creative dissertation.

A hint that that there might be more than one way to craft my "creative" dissertation came during a class I took with poet and scholar Hunt Hawkins entitled "Poesis." This course was billed as a "literary theory course for creative writers" and was designed with the assumption that many, if not most, creative writers found that literary theory subverts their perceptions of how language and writing works. Reading Derrida, Foucault, Kristeva, and others was daunting to be sure, but I found myself fascinated. While many of my classmates thought theory to be intimidating and antagonistic, I felt liberated by the idea that I really had little or no control over the language I used in my poems, that the language was as alive as I was, and that each reader breathed new life into a text with every reading. I was giddy with the riches of possibility that poststructuralist theory had bestowed on my poor little poems. And so I took the first steps in creating my nontraditional dissertation, "The Hermeneutics of Birdsong," a scholarly creative hybrid that ultimately would be both shunned and embraced and that would cause my supervisory committee to fracture and reform.

Inspired by my theory class, I began writing poems that explored various aspects of language. I know it sounds odd to write poems with titles like "The Best Little Verb in the World," "Hold a Page Up to Your Lips and Blow," and "Seeking Comfort in the Dictionary," but I did and had fun doing so. Bolstered by actually being able to write poems about language and theory, I thought of expanding my project to include more theory but in a less obvious way: I would interweave poetic and rhetorical theory into a book of poems. Using epigraphs, footnotes, endnotes, and parallel text, I hoped to create a resonance between the poems and the theory that would inform and expand a reader's experience of each, and allow me to show off all that I had learned. At times, I shaped quotes from theorists into poems. Or I would footnote a poem not with an expected critical explication or aside, but with another poem.

By including rhetorical and literary theory in my poetry collection, I hoped to assuage the fears of any hiring committee that might wonder if I was just another beret-wearing creative writing flake who had coasted through graduate school. I also felt the need personally and intellectually to establish a context and depth for my poems that merely collecting them into a book would not provide. I wanted to prove to myself that I could not only use language poetically but also that I understood the forces at work to shape my ideas of authorship, genre, and meaning-making.

My First Major Professor, a long-time poet and champion of the local writing community, was not pleased I had "stunk up such sweet poems with all that theory crap." While he didn't come right out and say no to the idea of expanding my poetry collection to include critical and metacommentary, his lack of enthusiasm was evidenced in the blank looks, indifferent comments, and missed appointments I endured for a good year after my comps. I was somewhat surprised that there was such a narrow notion of what constituted a "creative" dissertation afoot at FSU. After much thought and secret negotiations with another professor whom I had learned was interested in hybrid genres and who graciously agreed to take me on, I parted ways with My First Major Professor.

Viewed from the safety of the tenure-track position I now hold, this break with My First Major Professor amazes me. Fraught with anxiety over being considered disloyal to the creative writing community in the department, I nonetheless felt that remaining with this dissertation supervisor would not allow me the freedom to break with tradition—in this case to produce something other than a standard collection of poetry—and challenge myself as a writer and a scholar. Standing outside his office door the day I stopped by to give him the news, I felt like a young man who was about to tell his father he would not follow in his footsteps and join the family business. With knuckles poised to strike I hesitated a good while, but finally knock I did, not only on his door but against the very notion of what it meant to be a creative writer in the department.

My New Major Professor, herself both a theorist and a poet, was enthusiastic and full of helpful advice about my nontraditional poetry collection. This encouragement was heady indeed, and I felt liberated and legitimized by this support. While encouraging my experimentation with voice and form, this professor's careful reading also kept me on my toes, making sure that my commentary was not only interesting and legitimate in its theoretical and historical assertions, assumptions, and questions but also that it worked well to complement my poetry so that the whole—poems and commentary—came together as a comprehensible text. Buoyed with this professor's support, I rose above my doubts and continued to experiment and explore. Only on the eve of my defense did I worry that I—we—had gone too far!

Since I was delving into multiple worlds—creative writing, literary theory, poetics, and rhetoric—I had left myself open to multiple avenues of attack by any committee members who had an axe to grind or a real concern about my poems or commentary. I was keenly aware that any one of them could send me back to the drawing board by refusing to accept my hybrid manuscript as a legitimate work. One very awkward moment came during the defense when an often-published poet on my committee, after commenting on the learned and original qualities of my dissertation, asked, "Of what use is such a dissertation?"

Stunned, my initial reaction was a wide-eyed stare and silence. The other committee members shifted nervously in their padded conference room chairs or averted their eyes from my now suspect manuscript. Someone laughed nervously. No one looked at me. While a variety of less-than-academic responses coursed through my mind as my blood pressure mounted, I decided to answer as if the question had not left me feeling cut off at the knees and hobbling toward my own doom. Having gone through several years of confusion, a revolt against My First Major Professor, and two more years of work that challenged me as both a writer and intellectual, I was not going to back down now.

So I began to talk, letting one word latch onto another in a rapid stream-of-conscious mini-lecture that I hoped would rehabilitate my shamed manuscript. I explained how my dissertation sought to provide a theoretical and historical context for my poetry, to situate my own work in terms of past influences, to explore and analyze the conventions of the genre, and to examine my new understanding of the nature of language and meaning-making. I thought about adding that including the hypertext layer of commentary had made the project more fun for me, but decided I should keep that tidbit my own little secret. I realized later that this professor, considered a very fun and creative guy himself, was asking not so much about my own learning process or validation as a scholar but rather about a very real and traditional academic concern: whether the manuscript would appeal to an academic publisher.

Though I may never publish "The Hermeneutics of Birdsong" in its entirety, many of the individual poems and some of the critical notes have been published in various small magazines and journals. But most of all, my nontraditional dissertation allowed me to put into practice the best of the poetic, rhetorical, and literary theory I had spent years studying. It allowed me to do so in new and creative ways and to have fun doing it—what a way to learn! I ended my doctoral journey a little battered and bitter but with a dissertation that I am proud of and that I enjoyed creating.

Fracturing the Monolith: Conformity and Challenge

One department. Two dissertation writers. One dissertation director. Two distinct experiences. While our separate narratives illustrate our subjective experiences as dissertation writers, looking at our experiences together offers an insight to some of the greater forces at work within an English department and within the profession itself.

In "What Discourses Have in Common," Peshe Kuriloff (1996) investigates interactions between disciplinary discourses—interactions that became problems we both had to solve as writers of hybrid or blended genre dissertations. Starting from the position that "[w]riting is a form of social interaction" (486) and that "[t]hese social relationships look different in different types of writing" (492), Kuriloff goes on to argue that if we consider writing in the academy as a conversation, "[y]ou understand me because we have a relationship and because our conversation occurs in a context and follows principles with which both of us are familiar" (493). That's a claim our dissertation histories bear out as we attempted to forge relationships and conversations across contexts and their governing principles.

The strictures of genre did govern and control both our experiences, and our stories of dissertating dramatize Robert Scholes' (1985) assertion in *Textual Power* that "A genre is as real as a language and exerts similar pressures through its network of codes, meeting similar instances of stolid conformity and playful challenge" (2). Our dissertation experiences can also be read through that "dialectic" of "stolid conformity" and "playful challenge." Through blurring and blending genres, contexts, and relationships, each of us was necessarily more interested in and involved with play—with language, with genre—than the traditional dissertation writer. Each had to negotiate the play between an orderly process that would result in credentialing, and the carnival of codes—theory poems, criticism, and personal narratives—we introduced and considered integral to our products.

By willfully subverting genre boundaries, we also willfully subverted the monolithic facade of the department's and the profession's status quo. In the academy, as Nancy Mairs (1994) writes, "the genres are like armed camps, and transgressing their boundaries can result in swift expulsion" (24). Though grouped together in an uneasy alliance as a department, at our university the literature, composition, and creative writing camps each had clearly demarcated lines of authority, influence, and territory. While some few faculty members were allowed to traverse the tricky routes between concentrations, most were firmly entrenched—or imprisoned—within an area of specialty. Students, too, were directed, if not required, to declare allegiance to one camp or another: follow its dictates, conform to its practices, revel in the status it brought (creative writing) or bemoan its underappreciated and overutilized place (composition) within the department hierarchy. Our projects not only resisted entrenchment but also put back into play the question of what our professional identities, as creative writers, as compositionists, could be. The rhetorical situations of our dissertations, inscribed by genre, gender, and class, did differ greatly. Even so, we credit our director for "embracing contraries" at the doctoral level and helping us negotiate that dialectic between conformity and challenge. Through the process of writing with a supportive director while interrogating our disciplines, we learned something of how "to nullify the splitting—of body from spirit, of critic from creator, of intellect from desire, of self from other—characteristic of Western discourse . . ." (Mairs 1994, 36).

Thus we became credentialed in Western discourse while dissenting—in some ways—from the separations and stratifications it embodies. For both of us, the dissertation—finding the form and negotiating the situation—was more dialogue rather than monologue or monolith, a multivocal writing scene of open-ended inquiry despite our narratives' moments of limits and constraint. Our experiences suggest that the dissertation as writers actually experience it might more closely resemble an extended and learned exploration than a form-bound pronouncement: a *process* of interrogation rather than a written *product* or final report. As Winston Weathers observes, form is a principle, a process, and an experience rather than a thing, an object, or a shape (qtd. in Bishop 1997, 3). The dissertation process does exert strong pressures for conformity, but the nontraditional dissertation, as a site for both collaboration and dissensus, conformity and challenge, is helping to rewrite the process. If the traditional dissertation reifies the voice of the solitary masculine knower and the conventions—formal, social, and political—that enable its dominion, then the nontraditional dissertation suggests alternatives, disruptions, other voices.

Still, while our director helped both of us construct positions as writers that would allow us to be credentialed and to interrogate the credentialing process, our narratives also suggest that Darrell faced less committee interference and restriction in the process of assembling his dissertation. We wonder whether Darrell, by nature of his self-construction as a creative writer—a subdiscipline that in the English department hierarchy is placed above composition (Scholes 1985, 7)—simply had a bigger playground than Devan. According to Scholes, composition as traditionally defined produces (manufactures) "non-literature," thus constructing it as "other" in an English department that sees itself as consuming literature (7).

Both of us had spent most of our previous working lives in nonmanagerial positions: Darrell as a bartender, Devan as a postal clerk. The post office is perhaps a little more like a factory. Her work—she dumped, sorted, and boxed mail—was "physically demanding [and] repetitive" (5), a characteristic Tokarczyk and Fay (1993), in *Working-Class Women in the Academy,* ascribe to working-class jobs. In addition, Devan's work was "largely differentiated by . . . lack of autonomy. Clerical workers, factory employees, and other 'workers' are all closely supervised" (Tokarczyk and Fay 1993, 5). Darrell, while in a service job, remained in control behind the bar, with thirsty customers at the busy night spot vying for his favor and attention. As such, his role as provider—a traditional masculine role—granted him authority and prestige beyond that of most service workers.

Thus Devan, schooled as a woman in a blue-collar job and seeking entry into the "ghettoized" field of composition, learned that the post office and the academy, both institutions, operate in similar ways: Deviation from standard operating procedure is less accepted from someone with low status. The discipline's professionalization was meant to empower those who teach nonfiction prose writing, yet ironically, composition's moves toward disciplinary status may have occasioned the need for Devan to rewrite extensively, thus allowing her text to both honor and question convention but inadvertently reinscribing her post office identity as someone who "knows her place." Darrell, the bartending poet accustomed to greater control in performing his duties outside of school, forged ahead, arrogantly challenging his own dissertation director and the department's generic conventions for a creative dissertation.

Would our experiences within the department and with our committees have been different if Darrell had been a female creative writer and Devan a male compositionist?

Returning in disguise for another go at a doctorate might provide a hint of insight into these questions, but since it is unlikely that hell will freeze over, this mystery must remain.

Chapter Nine

The Multiple Voices in the Dissertation and Beyond

Janis E. Haswell

Is it irony or pathos that as successful candidates submit what should be their crowning achievement in English studies, too many feel cheated by the process? For some candidates, writing the dissertation seems an empty exercise, one final hoop to navigate. For others the process might seem worse, as figures in authority recommend changes, ostensibly for the good of the candidate, perhaps in reality mercenarily making sure that this particular side of beef is good enough to bear their brand in the job market. Linda Brodkey's (1989) term "discursive hegemony" may be appropriate in these cases, unhappily.

While such experiences are indefensible, they are not necessarily endemic or unavoidable. I would like to describe my own dissertation process, notable for two reasons. First my experience was indicative of work that becomes seed for the future. Second, because I defended eight years ago, the eventual result (a published book) is already known, which helps us to envision the dissertation as a point along a broader continuum. With this long-term perspective, I hope to show the value of the dissertation both as text and as process not readily apparent at the time of its writing. Lest the reader despair that the following pages will be merely a defense of the *ancien regime,* let me state outright that my purpose is less defensive than exploratory. I mean to analyze the dissertation as a crucial stage of what we as scholars and writers value perhaps as much as anything: how we develop our own professional voices. In my case, that voice could not exist without the very process this anthology addresses.

My story might seem ancillary to this collection, since my specialization is English literature. Yet issues of tradition versus innovation, master versus apprentice, ownership versus voice, emerge in the dissertation process across academic disciplines. Of these concerns I will focus on "voice," that pearl of great price. Composition theory has understood voice in different and complex ways, depending on what notion of self is in currency. For my purposes, it will be helpful to note the following stances.

1. The romantic/expressivist sense of voice was attributed to the self conceived (in Clifford Geertz's words) as a "bounded, unique, more or less integrated motivational and cognitive universe, a dynamic center of awareness" (Shweder and Bourne 1984, 167). This seamless self is capable of manifesting an "authentic" voice, one that is true, natural, and innate to the individual (Trilling 1972, 9).
2. The postmodern notion of voice stems from a vision of the self as a "subject" or field of cultural forces. Whether the subject can only register and absorb exterior influences, or whether the subject can resist those forces and exercise agency, voice emerges, as Charles Taylor believes, only in dialogue with other voices within the culture and "with the interanimation of its voices" (qtd. in Freisinger 1994, 271).
3. A third notion of voice might be called the feminist, rooted in a gendered notion of the self (gender variously defined—essentially, linguistically, or as a position within relations). Depending on the type of feminist perspective, this voice can be conceived as authentically female, as socioculturally constructed, or as a "rhetoric of radical possibility," as Susan Brown Carlton (1994) conceives of it, wherein an individual woman accommodates "the myriad discourse situations" she faces (236, 240).

To the credit of my dissertation committee, each of these components—a mature self, the bonds of a discourse community, and carefully selected rhetorical positions—provided the context for my voice to emerge. I would also add a final but vital component: Voice emerges when the writer has something to say. In this chapter I will argue that it is the function of the dissertation process to create a context for these four elements to converge. At the same time, it would be a mistake to regard the dissertation as a final stage rather than as the beginning of a process that does not end with the defense, but spills over into long-term outcomes.

To demonstrate how my voice emerged during this process, I will analyze three versions of the introduction to my dissertation. Version 1 was submitted to my committee after seven months of intensive reading. Version 2 is the introduction to the dissertation as defended, and Version 3 is the introduction as submitted to a university press before copy editing. For rhetorical purposes that will become clear later on, I'll narrate the next several sections in third person.

Version 1

This first attempt at an introduction seeks to establish the importance of Yeats's vision of gender in the context of contemporary feminist theory. Out of ten pages, the first five sketch a quick overview of the last twenty-five years of feminist literary criticism. Thirty-three feminist critics are named and nine theoretical positions are described. Except for the opening sentence, Yeats is not mentioned until the bottom of page five:

> Such issues might seem only as muddles to W. B. Yeats. The distinction between sex and gender would be only a feminist construct to him. There are males and females, he would insist, also called men and women, who naturally behave in certain masculine and feminine ways. Although they are not exclusive, masculine and feminine traits are distinct from each other and vital to human existence.

The writer goes on to argue that feminist analysis gives readers a lens to recognize the gender components of Yeats's world view better than Yeats himself could at the time, since he did not benefit from such insights as the distinction between sex and gender. The writer continues:

> But our understanding of Yeats is enhanced by making distinctions he did not make, between sex (the physical/biological makeup of males and females) and gender ("the particular cultural way in which one's biology is presented, understood and played out" [Farganis]). These distinctions will serve as filters to reveal how much Yeats himself constructed his own understanding of gender and how that construct infused his metaphysics and aesthetics.

Now the content takes a turn—the writer introduces the issue of Yeats's debt to those writers who had preceded him. The writer's argument is that Yeats's vision of gender is unique—more critics are cited from Yeats studies—and then comes the closest thing to a thesis statement:

> I will explore how Yeats's gendered world view produces a gendered language, what that language consists of, what it accomplishes, and how it is deployed in the mask.

But this forecast is more a dead end than an open door, as the writer succumbs to the pressure of displaying her grasp of current theory. Thus the reader is immediately directed to the "traps" of such a gendered vision rather than informed by a clarification or expansion of this claim.

The shortcomings in this version are obvious. It is a topic with no interpretive position or original insight, no organizing thesis. There is no voice, only an effort to capture what other authorities say. Or more accurately, if there is a voice here, it is the voice of an apprentice who feels the need to pay homage to a long legacy of critical discourse. Yet Version 1 is also exploratory as it seeks to navigate several critical and theoretical landscapes (Yeats studies, feminist criticism, gender studies) and raises for the writer the question of where she stands in these landscapes. Only one idea will survive from the exploration—that Yeats's sense of the duality between masculine and feminine is relational, not simply adversarial.

> Although Yeats believed that fundamental distinctions between masculine and feminine are sustained in life and in art, he conceives of the duality between male and female as relational rather than ontological. There is more to being male or female than biology.

Nearly ninety pages of exploration generated this single kernal of insight—an important insight because it provided the direction the writer would take with the final draft of the dissertation.

Version 2

The contrast between the initial draft of the introduction and the final version of the dissertation is startling. Replacing the epic catalogue of feminist scholars is a meager list of Yeats scholars, a passing nod to cultural critics who study the late nineteenth and early twentieth centuries, and a handful of gender theorists. In addition, the rationale for dealing with gender takes a far sharper focus as the writer links gender with Yeats's theory of the mask through the strange and rare being called the *daimon*—for Yeats an ontological reality buried within the human psyche. The attraction and discord between human being and daimon is analogous to the relationship between men and women. Seeing this link helps the writer conceive of gender in a new way:

> Gender is employed not only as a subject in [Yeats's] poetry, but as the means of fleshing out his philosophy and clothing his personal experiences in a universal and comprehensible metaphor. . . . Moreover, what Yeats calls "universal masculine and feminine" is imprinted upon all aspects of the human experience. . . . Gender determines the way Yeats views reality.

The writer's new appreciation of gender in Yeats's mature verse, rooted in Yeats's own metaphysical vision, finally evokes a clear argument. Because in 1919, Yeats's daimon is defined not only as ideal self or anti-self but also as *female,* the mask (that territory wherein daimon and poet battle for ascendancy) is a gendered and gendering action: "Thus the mask is not simply an aesthetic process. It is sexual in scope—a gendered union, an action that works toward a gendered whole. . . ." The introduction closes by placing this claim in the context of feminist discourse, the writer arguing that while current gender theory does not accommodate Yeats's vision of gender, the poet should not be considered unenlightened.

Here is new ground, but the writer is not comfortable in claiming it. If the first draft conveyed the voice of an apprentice, this version enacts the voice of an observer who can see beyond pieces to patterns, but a voice that still has severe limitations. Perhaps *limitations* isn't the right word—it is more a burden that the writer carries, one hundred years of critical commentary that she has been expected to master along with the Yeats corpus itself. Because the writer is intent on being original, she is forced to assume a defensive posture: "Feminist definitions of gender cannot capture what Yeats describes as 'universal masculine and feminine,' or how they work to mold reality." Believing herself to be surrounded and alone, she is a writer at bay, determined to take a stand under the flag of her thesis. Rather than building on tradition, she tries consciously to challenge it. Yet she also must show that she is accountable to the sources everyone expects her to cite. There are thirteen critics cited in six pages and a notable amibivalence toward other feminists. How to genuflect and rebel at the same time? This is the mare's nest of the initiate, but not the end of the story.

Version 3

In the final version of the introduction, there is a sense of confidence and purpose previously absent. The thesis and its rationale are more specific, the discussion more focused. Such tightening is grounded in the writer's extensive use of a new Yeatsian source, the full Automatic Script materials that had just recently become available. The Script provides crucial insights into the emergence of Yeats's "double-voiced verse," and in terming Yeats's postscript verse as double-voiced, the writer looks beyond Yeats's daimonic theory—what in the dissertation served as the foundation to his theory of the mask—to his theory of the self and the Four Faculties, now radically defined and rooted in the contrasexual daimon.

Two results flow naturally from this conceptual breakthrough. First, the writer has a clear motivation—Yeats's own radical reconceptualization of the mask—for her the revisionist readings. Second, the earlier feeding frenzy of citations disappears. Her swath of critics is now limited to those scholars who (1) study Yeats and address his double-voiced poetry, but do not take into account the Script materials, or (2) study the issue of multivocality and gender in literature but do not take note of Yeats's idiosyncratic approach. In this introduction of twenty pages, there are only six critics cited, all for specific reasons. Moreover, the writer argues that rather than mining Yeats's masks for the "real" man, scholars can enlarge current theories of subjectivity through Yeats's radical vision of the bisexual ego:

> Perhaps more than any other poet of our century, Yeats deliberately and self-consciously works within a sense of the fictional self, generating multiple masks that create for readers a flexible network of selves. . . . If for no other reason, the implications of this study extend beyond Yeatsian scholarship. . . . the act of masking and the exercise of gender are hardly [Yeats'] exclusive domain.

Clearly, the writer has labored to the very paradox that justifies her revisionist reading: Yeats's vision of self and voice proves relevant to contemporary theory while, at the same time, his radical conception of gender cuts against the grain of current feminist and gender theory. In articulating this insight, the writer is more than an apprentice, more than an observer. Here is a professional, even personalized voice that "owns" and argues her position.

Texts and Contexts: The Role of the Dissertation Committee

Because it is difficult to gauge whether my institution is typical in terms of how graduate faculty deal with students and with each other, I cannot evaluate whether my experience is rare or representative. Newly hired faculty often remarked about the collegial atmosphere of the department, and I benefited from the faculty's willingness to accommodate my needs (as an older, returning student with a family and a long commute) in terms of teaching schedule, committee duties, and so on. What I *am* sure about is my good fortune in receiving the kind of mentoring that proves invaluable, thanks to the skills and integrity of my chair and committee members. As is evident from the previous discussion, the initial draft of the dissertation could easily have generated enough negative response to rout whatever confidence and interest I had in the project. Worse yet, committee members could have advised me in such a way that my draft would be turned into theirs. They did neither. Instead, they walked the fine line between allowing me the latitude to explore the full potential of my project and leading me through or around impediments both in my writing and in my thinking.

This is not to say that all ran smoothly. In the first year of writing, four of my five committee members either left for sabbatical or retired, and the fifth member (my chair) resigned without warning. I would go through another chair (he took a job elsewhere) before finding a third who would go the distance with me and help form a new committee the second year. My relationship with this committee was never adversarial, to the credit of my chair during that second year, Tim Hunt, who believed his role was to ensure that problems were diverted before they ever touched me.

Since Tim worked at a branch campus some 300 miles away, we spent long hours on the phone, in part discussing passages in the chapter under construction, in part strategizing the next chapter still to take shape. But if memory serves me right, much of our conversations were therapeutic rather than directive in the sense that Tim helped me first to envision a readership with expectations, knowledge, and interests, then to find the confidence to write as a full-fledged member of that same readership. What evolved through those exchanges wasn't just a text but a way of reenvisioning myself as a scholar and, subsequently, of understanding how to speak and relate to the profession, my ultimate audience.

During the first year of writing, my understanding of audience was limited to the committee itself, which helps explain why Version 1 was so saturated with the voices of other scholars. I was playing to individual committee members who brought their various specialties to the project. The reaction of the committee was predictable, to some extent. Because this section was front-loaded with feminists, the Yeatsian asked to see more Yeats criticism, while the nineteenth-century scholar requested more discussion of Yeats's historical context. Despite these varied perspectives, members were united in their concern that the draft was mired in theoretical issues too distant from Yeats himself. After reading this first introduction and companion chapters, they agreed that I should rewrite, "condensing this Introduction and parts of Chapters II–III into a new introduction more centered on Yeats." A clear, positive sense of direction, and a kind way of pointing out that the bulk of this draft needed to be pruned away.

In their advice after my defense, with the publication of a book version in mind for the future, committee members suggested repositioning material so that my own theoretical position and assumptions were more explicit. After a series of specific instructions, one member wrote:

> Actually, in your dissertation you have done all this already—that is, you have the material and the theory—you just don't make it explicit, or rather don't take this way explicitly as your scholarly approach. If you did, it would help sell the book to scholars.

The pivotal shift to writing for the wider audience of the profession was one of the final stages of the process, possible only after the dissertation was completed. During long months of moving from dissertation to monograph, I also entered the academic world as an assistant professor. The audience I had previously only imagined were now my colleagues. I could put faces to names I had cited and had a better sense of what teachers-as-scholars want and expect.

Through the dramatic changes in my committee, the turnover of chairs, the logistics of distance mentoring, and the normal worries, I had to take on faith that the process was a good one. Now I know this to be the case. Admittedly, my positive experience is grounded in the dedication and good sense of my committee members, who brought together two of those components vital to voice. They initiated me into a discourse community (composed first of the committee itself, then of the larger profession) and encouraged the development of carefully selected rhetorical skills to employ within that community.

Texts and Contexts: The Dissertation Writer

And what of those final two components: a mature self with something to say?

As I reflect now on my own experience, I have the advantage of knowing that the insights and arguments of my dissertation continued to develop, with five years of hard work, into a published book. Although there is very little left of the draft I defended in its final form, the two works are inseparably bound together. If (as we tell our student writers) the process is as important as the product, those two years as a dissertation writer were a constructive and indispensable factor in my professional achievement and personal growth. My dissertation proved more than a last hurdle to the PhD. It is a part of a continuum that extends into the future and is rooted in my past.

Hindsight can sometimes glide over chuckholes of memory without much jostling, but from where I sit now, the value of the process is inarguable. This is precisely the advantage of leaving some judgments until the continuum has revealed the value of a given experience. It is a principle after Virginia Woolf's own heart, I admit—the meaning of an event keeps unraveling, and therefore interpreting that event cannot be done hastily or simplistically.

Such unraveling extends into the future, surely, but also back through the past. Every text is inexorably linked to its context. Every text has a story (or several stories) behind it. To tell the story of my dissertation, I would have to begin years before my entry into graduate school. Like many of us, I always wanted to write. I grew up with a father who at one point quit his job to write, stealing away to the den for hours on end to pen the great American short story. In the fourth grade, I tried my hand at a new line of "Black Stallion" books. But I soon discovered that Walter Farley's talent exceeded mine. Years later in high school, as I read Walter Kerr on Sophocles, I realized I would never write an *Oedipus Rex*—I couldn't even write *The Black Stallion Returns*. But I might write a *Tragedy and Comedy*. Twenty-four years later, the dissertation proved a formative stage in that quest to find my niche as an academic and my voice as a literary critic. Formative but not final.

As the acquisition editor perused my manuscript, as Yeats scholars reviewed my book, and (hopefully) as teachers found the end product a useful tool in their courses, they worked with only a portion of the story—the public text—apart from its personal but crucial context, as vital to the product as the dissertation process itself. In most instances, the three texts described in the first part of this chapter would also stand alone, the absence or presence of voice within those texts being judged by individual readers who do not have access to the contexts. But in terms of the theme of this collection— *The Dissertation and the Discipline: Reinventing Composition Studies*—I have a unique opportunity to flesh out the contexts of those texts. Hence the move from impersonal, third-person analysis in the first sections, to personal, first-person narrative in this one.

In my case, there is a paradox embedded in the meeting point between text and context. While I struggled to find my voice in these various drafts, I was never haunted by a sense of "speechlessness," as some of my colleagues have been. There is an important distinction between feeling silenced and working through the process of cultivating a unique voice for a new and particular purpose. Perhaps waiting for fifteen years between completing my BA in history and starting a masters in English helped me appreciate how liberating to the mind and heart academic discourse can be. The contrast between functioning as a wife and mother and meeting scholarly demands of the intellectual world made me feel like I had come back to life. I am not belittling the role of caregiver here, only pointing out that for many women, nurturing does not bring with it many opportunities to claim or develop their own voice(s). Even when a woman sustains intellectual interests and pursuits in the home (I had coauthored and published a monograph during this period), much of her energy is dedicated to activities far afield from demands of intellectual life, such as expressing thoughts in writing or articulating insights in a classroom discussion. Coming back to the academic world, I was dazzled by the multiple opportunities to speak and be heard.

As a woman, I did not feel speechless or silenced by what Lillian Bridwell-Bowles (1992), Don Kraemer (1991), Rae Rosenthal (1995), Patrocinio P. Schweickart (1990), and Terry Zawacki (1992) (among others), have labeled the masculine world of academic discourse. But certainly my case is not typical. There was the fifteen-year hiatus, for one. Because of it, I enjoyed a long honeymoon period in graduate school. For me, it wasn't an endless grind laced with grueling demands or senseless exercises, as I had been forewarned. True, I paid the piper in other ways, having to be cruelly disciplined, not being the best mother because I was a student, not the best student because I was a mother, commuting eighty miles one way for four years across isolated wheat fields that in a winter storm could white out with eerie beauty. My biggest fear was failing, leaving school, and returning to an intellectually dormant state.

How does my personal context this complex continuum of past, present, and future—shed light on the current debate about voice in composition studies? In part, I have tried to answer Toby Fulwiler's (1994) question, "Did you ever try and locate your own voice?" (158). It is a tricky business, indeed. In the first part of this chapter, I have worked *to* voice by analyzing successive texts. In this second part, I am working *from* voice to the person who developed it, possesses it, and hones it—a far more difficult job but one that teachers face with each writer (graduate or undergraduate) in their classrooms—and who does not simply produce texts but works out of a specific context, proceeding along his or her own continuum. Who is this self behind the voice? By examining the contexts of my dissertation drafts, I am perforce rejecting the view of some postmodernists that academic discourse is produced by an individual who is first absorbed into a discourse community and then assumes the subject position of an academic. What I brought to the seminar table or to the printed page or to my own texts was more than an individual at that precise juncture of the continuum. Not only did I ferry back and forth between two worlds eighty miles apart (my private life and my academic life), I connected those worlds. I enlarged who I was and, in turn, brought those many selves to my academic voice(s). As Yeats pointed out, dualities (like personal and academic voice) are more relational than adversarial. I wrote out of my continuum, and still do.

Even so, I struggled to find and craft my voice as a writer. I think it was for two reasons, evident with hindsight and connected to the same question we ask of student writers: What is the relation of this writer in this text to her audiences? As already noted, I had no conception of audience beyond my classroom teachers and peers. Until I could visualize my place in the profession and enter into a relationship with my academic audiences, I would not develop my own voice. The second reason complicates this first. For not only did I have to overcome the mindset of being a graduate student and initiate, but also of being *just* a wife or *just* a mother, or *just* an older, returning student.

Oddly, Yeats himself struggled with the same issue, although in different terms. Initially, he believed the poetic voice should be highly symbolic, focused on the abstract, expressed by exceptional and finely crafted (read *tortured*) language. Very soon, however, he realized that he couldn't touch other hearts apart from a voice that reflected normal, everyday speech. But does normal speech reflect the "real" person? Ultimately for Yeats, no. In fact, poetry most often projects the opposite of the authentic self, so that Keats (a man Yeats saw as imprisoned by poverty, ignorance, and poor health) thirsted for luxury and generated "imaginary delights"; Walter Savage Landor wrote with calm nobility out of the "daily violence of his passion" (Yeats 1959, 326, 328–29). In his endless search for expression, Yeats's final discovery was of a contrasexual ego, personified in a female daimon who was "part of me" (1992) and who compelled him to develop a voice that at various times expressed "the woman in me" (1964).

Ultimately, Yeats was faithful to his mystical vision, insisting to the end that his occult materials were the foundation of his poetry. In that sense, he resisted most of the intellectual, social, and cultural forces of his time—intentionally so—since he saw such forces as part of the "murderousness" of the world (1965). At the same time, he realized that while his readers might hunger for poetry from this perspective, they would in turn be resistant to its mystical underpinnings. Thus Yeats made sure (after a few very philosophical poems he later regretted writing) that no hint of his personal philosophy (or the context to his texts) was evident in his plays and poems. "My 'private philosophy' is there but there must be no sign of it," he insisted. "It guides me to certain conclusions and gives me precision but I do not write it" (1954, 918).

From this perspective, Yeats isn't so different from me or from my students. He adjusted the language and even the content of his poetry to appeal to his audience. Yet behind the text is Yeats in his own continuum, imbued in a very personal context of mystical experimentation, engulfing him in an ambiguous relationship with his female daimon while formulating and enacting a radical and complex vision of gender and of the self. Can readers work backward *from* Yeats's voice to the person who developed it, possessed it, and honed it? In my book, I argue that we must, and luckily, the Automatic Script (among other sources) enables us to do so.

Peeling away the layers of dissertation drafts provides a second insight nearly too obvious to state, yet in the numerous theoretical analyses and discussions about voice, I have yet to see anyone allude to it. What is the relation between voice and content? Developmentalists have long observed the connection between mature stages of intellectual development and the ability to articulate a thesis with a distinct, unifying voice. Rich Haswell (1991), Janice Hays (1987), and Melanie Hanson (1986) are good examples. But I am suggesting a more direct link here. Even though a certain maturity level must be reached before a writer is willing to own a position, there must also be material worth owning. I didn't develop a voice (beyond the apprentice) until I had something to say. Something to say—apart from audience, apart from style of discourse or rhetorical choices—a message. For seven years I worked with Yeats's Script materials, his theosophical essays, his plays, his poetry, and a mountain of Yeatsian scholarship. After defending what in this story is called Version 2, I produced four successive, complete drafts. With each one, I was deepening my grasp of the material, understanding its ramifications, internalizing and growing confident in my insights, and better articulating what I recognized and comprehended. I was in pursuit of a message beyond something original or confrontational, beyond an academic or political agenda, yet within my own capabilities.

My ability to relate to an academic audience, to comprehend and internalize complex material and its ramifications, to reflect on feminists' responses to issues, and honestly face and articulate my own—all this is bound up in the continual process of reimagining myself as a teacher and scholar in more confident and integrative ways, and to the exploratory and epistemic process of drafting, revising, and reconceiving the subject matter and my relationship to it. Only then was I able to withhold nothing in terms of effort, thinking, and interrogation of the material, ultimately doing justice to my sources—and finding something to say, and a voice.

Justice is a good word here. What I learned by studying and writing about Yeats helps me understand my own continuum. If I justly represent these insights, then what I write today as a literary critic (to be read in the future, within someone else's continuum) should ring true, just as Walter Kerr's words did for me years ago. Rather than being self-serving, as I sometimes found it in graduate school, academic writing can be a bridge whereby readers can access and identify with other texts and contexts. Perhaps that is the basic meaning of *voice:* Yeats *speaks* to me. Yeats speaks *to me*. As an academic, I can help others access Yeats's texts and context, or (in the case of this essay) allow others to share in my own.

Considering the dissertation as a single point on the continuum enables me to interpret that point for what it really is—a once-in-a-lifetime opportunity to be mentored by a senior colleague I trusted and to learn in at least a collective if not collaborative mode with my committee members, in order to produce what would not be the definitive study of my life but only the initial stage of a project that proved to be worth years of effort and dedication. Of course this story (and my continuum) does not end here. The committee is replaced by editors, critics, and colleagues. I've dedicated myself to other projects, and found new and (I hope) better voices in the process. And *this* text will build on the work of others, others will respond to this text, and the dialogue that yields fruitful understanding will continue.

Chapter Ten

The Personal Narrative in Dissertation Writing

A Matter of Academic Honesty

Tonya M. Stremlau

It is a matter of academic honesty to admit potential bias in scholarship. Our personal experiences bias us in all sorts of ways. We know and should admit this. But where is it appropriate to include the personal in scholarly writing? When is it all right to step out of the formal, objective, scholarly voice (like this one) into the more informal *I* voice of narrative? For a book chapter like this, or a journal article, it is fairly acceptable to use personal narrative. It would not be out of order for me to tell you that this chapter evolved from a Conference on College Composition and Communication (CCCC) workshop presentation when I was near the end of writing my dissertation, that my perspective on my dissertation and this chapter has—not surprisingly—changed as I moved from graduate student to professor. I could even write that doing the final revision for this chapter has been very difficult because trying to think about this general topic—the intersection of personal experience and scholarship—pulls my mind to the murders of two students in their dorm rooms on my campus this academic year. One of the young men, Benjamin Varner, had been a student in my fall composition class where I taught students that their personal experiences should be written about. I know I learned a lot about Ben from his writing, and I wonder how much he learned about himself. I teach students to use personal experience because I believe it will empower writing for them as it did for me; it empowered my dissertation, "Deaf Students in Mainstreamed College Composition Courses: Culture and Pedagogy."

Since I completed my dissertation, personal experience has continued to be the focus of my scholarly activity. For example, I have been frustrated as a writer and a teacher by the scarcity of published deaf fiction writers to teach to my classes or to use as inspirations for my own writing. It disturbs me that for one of the courses I teach, "The Deaf in Literature," I can easily find deaf characters in books by hearing writers (portrayals that even when positive rarely ring true to me as a deaf reader) while I face difficulty in balancing these with deaf fiction writers. So I go to the special collection in the Gallaudet University library, the Deaf Stacks, where I find published creative writing by deaf authors, mostly out of print. I assign more creative writing and do more of it myself. I am now getting ready to write my first paper on this work of finding and promoting creative writing by deaf authors, and I would not even consider trying to keep personal narrative out of it. This approach—recognizing and acknowledging the personal experiences that give rise to the questions I investigate in research—seems natural now. However, acknowledging personal experience did not seem natural to me at all when I started the research that became my dissertation.

Most people who read my dissertation have expressed surprise over how much I emphasized my own experiences as a deaf person. It did not start out that way. Prior to writing my dissertation I tried to avoid using the first person or personal narrative in any scholarly writing. As an English major, I was well trained to present evidence from texts that I could quote and make all of my arguments follow logically. The graduate seminar paper that was the seed for my dissertation barely mentioned, much less stressed, that I was deaf. In fact, I mentioned it only to establish that I knew how hard it was not to have any deaf role models. At the time, I felt that even this mention—admitting that I had such a high personal stake in raising awareness of deaf issues in the teaching of English—undermined my writing. So how did I move from that perspective to using personal narratives as a framework for my dissertation?

The seminar paper that became the basis for my dissertation was not a bad paper, but when I wrote it and later when I presented a version of it at CCCC, I was dissatisfied with it. I was not sure why. My professor seemed to like it, and she encouraged me to think about how I could transform the topic—how culture affects the written English learning of deaf students—into a dissertation. In spite of the positive feedback, I was frustrated. There were so many things I wanted to say on the topic that I could not say while maintaining my stance of objectivity.

I look back at that paper, and I see how thoroughly I was trained to depend on logos—that is, to convince my readers through the logic of my propositions and conclusions. I very carefully structured an argument that compared the impact of the dominant (hearing) culture on deaf students to the impact of the dominant (white) culture on black students through issues like lowered expectations, the likelihood of facing discrimination in the job market, and school segregation. Finally, two pages from the end of the paper, I "slip" and mention that I am deaf: "I know from experience that it is difficult and frightening to envision oneself taking on a career in which one has no role models." That's it, and even there I see myself working very hard—through language choice—to maintain a careful, objective scholarly voice.

The summer after I wrote that paper, I embarked on an independent study, reviewing deaf education literature with a focus on literacy learning. Since I was not trained in deaf education, I wanted to learn all I could while getting the sources I would need as a foundation for my dissertation. Different schools of thought on deaf education all produced research supporting their approaches, and when I started, I had hoped I would find a magic bullet, the one approach that worked. I gave up on that search when I realized that the issue was too complex; my goal became to present and explain the complexity I found. As I read, I could not help considering what I knew from my experiences that supported or contradicted the books and articles. I had strong emotional reactions as well, including anger at myself for having accepted limitations on my own education. I kept reminding myself that I was not an expert and needed to focus on what those who were experts had to say. They had conducted studies, collected data, compiled statistics. In other words, they had the kind of information I trusted. Yet the more I read, the more I wondered which experts I could believe. I would need to figure out how to explain the contradictions. I would also need to figure out how to overcome my biases, to prevent myself from censoring or negatively presenting information that upset me personally.

This dependence on logos continued in my prospectus, which I wrote more than a year later. The first mention of my deafness in my twenty-page prospectus came at the end of page six. To explain what I wanted to do in my second chapter, "The Deaf Experience," I wrote, "At first, after I lost my hearing to spinal meningitis when I was ten, I thought that being deaf just meant that I could not hear any more. However, I soon found out that many people—even professionals (doctors, audiologists, educators) who work with the deaf—have preconceived ideas of what deaf people are like and how they should live."

Though this brief statement didn't come for six pages, it suggests what I had become convinced of in the interval between writing the seminar paper and completing my prospectus: that personal experience not only had a place in scholarship but also is sometimes necessary. I knew it was possible, of course, for me to write a dissertation on my topic without even mentioning that I was deaf or limiting such information to a preface or introduction. I could, but I didn't want to. I knew from my reading that relatively few deaf voices were present in the literature on deafness and deaf education, much less present in composition studies. Although many hearing people have done wonderful work in the field, I felt (and still feel) that many of the gaps I saw in existing research are there because so much of the work has been done by hearing people.

To take but one example, while doing my research I read Jacqueline Anderson's (1993) *Deaf Students Mis-Writing, Teacher Mis-Reading: English Education and the Deaf College Student.* Anderson's study, her doctoral dissertation, is a linguistics-based error analysis of deaf writers in college coupled with suggestions on how teachers can help such deaf students. She does a comprehensive, thorough job. Her choices about what to write are, however, very much those of a hearing person. Throughout her book, she makes statements such as "[T]he methods suggested are equally applicable to hearing students, and can be utilized in any mainstream, ESL, or English for Special Purposes classroom" (18). I had to wonder why, if the deaf students' writing errors, and the solutions to them, were like those for hearing students, she was separating deaf students as a group for her study. This is an important consideration because deaf people have long been grouped by hearing people based on deficiency.

My dissertation presents a different picture, one that shows the problems deaf students face with English resulting from the way (hearing) society is set up to favor hearing people. I explained in the preface my reasons for wanting to represent my self (my deaf self) in my dissertation:

> I want other teachers to be able to hear the concerns of a deaf student, one who happens to be training as a college composition teacher. My stories form an essential part of this text. Most writing on deaf education and deaf writing has been done by hearing people, since for the past hundred years hearing people have formed the voice of authority in the education of the deaf at all levels. Hearing professionals do have a valuable contribution to make, and I quote from them in my text. Deaf voices need to be heard too, though; mine is one. (Johnson, 1996, vi)

This argument about the need for deaf voices was important to me, and (I believe) was central in convincing my committee that my approach was valid.

In other words, I felt like my personal narrative was important, not just for what it said, but to remind my readers who was saying it. In an article on the issue of representation in qualitative composition research, Brenda Jo Brueggemann (1996) writes, "What difference, I ask, does it make *who* researches, *who* writes about, *who* represents 'subjects' in composition research?" (17). My answer, like Brueggemann's, is that it is very important. The further I got into my dissertation research and writing, the more certain I became that I was writing what I was writing because I am a deaf person who had spent many years in mainstreamed classrooms. My decision to use my personal narratives as a framework for the other information presented in my dissertation was based primarily on this conviction. My topic was so connected to my life that not to write about how my life and scholarship overlapped would have left out too much of the information my readers would need to judge what I had to say. In this sense, including my narratives became a matter of academic honesty.

I did continue to have concerns about the desirability of including personal experience in academic research. After all, personal experience is just that—personal, and therefore different than anyone else's. Can that be a basis for academic argument? I wondered: Does being part of a group that has been silenced in the academic world somchow give me more of a right to use my personal experience in academic writing? What if I were writing about something that was not deafness-related?

This question—whether it's necessary to be a representative of a specific group in order to use personal experience—concerned me because I knew, much more than my committee did, that there is no typical deaf person, no norm of voice or experience. There is wide variation, for instance, in degree and type of hearing loss, age of onset, and communication systems used. In addition, further differences could be attributed to family background (deaf or hearing, signing or nonsigning) and whatever education method(s) the deaf student had experienced during his or her school years. In my case, that means a postlingual total sensioneural hearing loss at age ten, communication mainly in English supplemented with the American Sign Language I began learning when I was eighteen, a hearing and nonsigning family, and a mainstreamed, oral education. Changing just one of those elements—say to a prelingual hearing loss—would have significantly changed what it means for me to be deaf. Thus my justification for using personal narrative had to go beyond the fact that I was a deaf person writing on deafness.

The research method that seemed closest to what I would do with my personal experience was the case study, in this instance a case study of myself. I introduced this focus in my dissertation immediately after making my argument about the importance of a deaf "voice." I quoted from Thomas Newkirk's "The Narrative Roots of the Case Study" that case-study narratives have a place as a knowledge-making tool because they have "capacity for detailed and individual accounts" (1992, 132). I wrote that "by turning my own experience as a mainstreamed deaf student into a case study, I hope my readers better understand what it is like to be a deaf student in predominantly hearing classes. However, I also know that my experience as a deaf student is in many ways far from typical. Therefore, I have introduced other experiences into my narrative" (Johnson, 1996, vi). Here, even as I make my case for using the personal and the subjective, I do not try to argue that the subjective should stand alone. I mix what is admittedly subjective—my memories and feelings—with (more) objective evidence such as publishcd education research. Each can inform the other, creating a final product that is richer through not neglecting potential ways of making meaning.

Although I did not make this argument in my dissertation itself, I also felt that Stephen North's support in *The Making of Knowledge in Composition* (1987) for using lore as a research tool could apply to what I was doing with my experiences. Of course, my lore was not teacher-lore but student-lore and culture-lore. If teacher experience in the classroom is worthy of research, however, surely student experience should be as well. Though I could not go back and set up my life as a controlled study—all I could do was look at and analyze my memories—I also could not hope to spend so much time with another subject. Only someone who has been through a mainstreamed education can understand (often only in retrospect) how much a deaf student misses—both "insignificant" information like where the weekend parties would be, as well as significant classroom instruction.

A personal story can make this point much more clearly and more memorably than technical descriptions of interpreters' limitations (since even the best have to make choices about what competing auditory information to present to the deaf client) or statistical analysis of what a hearing parent does and doesn't convey to a deaf child at the dinner table. A story encourages the reader to empathize, and the goal of my dissertation was for hearing teachers to understand what it means to be a deaf student in a hearing classroom. Here is that story:

My generation's equivalent of "Where were you when you heard JFK was shot?" is "Where were you when you learned about the Challenger explosion?" I remember very clearly. I was with my friends Kathy and Cindy in the snack food aisle at the Winn Dixie across the street from my high school at lunch time, looking for something tastier (if less nutritious) than what was being served in the cafeteria. Kathy said something about not feeling very hungry, and I asked her why. She said that she was upset by the Challenger exploding. I had to ask her to repeat what she had said, not sure if I was seeing clearly what her lips seemed to be saying. When she said the same thing again, I said, "The Challenger exploded?" I wouldn't believe them at first, sure they were pulling an appallingly tasteless joke. (It would fit; we had convinced Kathy the previous year that the black rubber bracelets that were suddenly popular—thanks to Madonna—were able to ward off cancer.) They finally convinced me that it was real and that our principal had made an announcement over the school intercom. I got very angry that no one had told me. How could everyone in my class fail to tell me something so significant?

That is what it means to be deaf.

Certainly there are problems with validity and reliability in personal experience, but there are similar problems in other forms of qualitative research. In addition, a quick glance through our field's books and journals shows that personal narrative is an accepted means of knowledge-making in composition and rhetoric. Why should dissertations be arbitrarily limited from accepted norms in scholarly conversation?

Yes, I understand that the dissertation must satisfy a set committee. If an article or a book is rejected by one set of readers, the author can try to find another publisher. A dissertation writer does not have that luxury. My committee expected me to balance my personal narrative with data from field and library research. When my dissertation was nearly complete, my codirectors stated that for my next draft to be acceptable, I needed to place more emphasis on published scholarship and the data I compiled from observing and talking to deaf students and their teachers. I followed their directions, finding more ways to weave in this information. I also expanded my reporting of what I observed in classes at the Louisiana School for the Deaf, the mainstream program at Baton Rouge's Robert E. Lee High School, and composition classes with mainstreamed deaf students at Louisiana State University.

It's not that the scholarship and field data were unimportant to me; not only had I invested a lot of time in them, but they had helped me think through my own experiences and reaffirmed my conviction that the work I was doing was important. However, I felt it was those aspects—the literature review and the research—that my committee chairs needed to determine whether my dissertation was worthy of a PhD. They wanted proof that I could gather data both from the field and from the library, and write them up in acceptable format. Their comments throughout the process, from the initial drafts of my prospectus to my defense, reminded me that it was their job to make sure that my dissertation fell within the established dissertation conventions. Those conventions are not spelled out anywhere, but even without written rules, dissertations form a predictable genre. Before embarking on my own, I paged through past humanities dissertations in the library at Louisiana State University to see what other people had done. They were all so scholarly, so serious . . . so like graduate seminar papers! The personal *I* was limited to the acknowledgments page.

The absence of the personal *I* should not be surprising. Its inclusion is taboo, viewed as dirty, contaminated with subjectivity. One published study, "Conventions, Conversations, and the Writer: Case Study of a Student in a Rhetoric Ph.D. Program" (Berkenkotter et al. 1988) describes how a graduate student in a rhetoric program becomes socialized to the conventions of writing in the field. The study measures the adjustment of the student, Nate, to the conventions of the composition and rhetoric discourse community, including his decreasing use of *I* in papers over the course of his first academic year. The study itself is a perfect example of academic social science writing; the *I* voice of Nate is suppressed except for quotations from his writing collected in the study. Why does Nate have to be presented to us in this way? Why can't Nate simply tell us his story and analyze his experience? After his year of training, Nate would have been unable to! His professor required him to get rid of that personal *I,* to stop drawing on his experiences to explain what he was learning in his courses. Although Nate's professor is more hard-line on this issue than others—some professors do not insist on the removal of *I* from all academic writing—the stereotype of academic writing, that "scientific" objective voice of fact and logic, remains. And dissertations are the ultimate in academic writing.

Others have already acknowledged that the personal has a place in both composition and rhetoric and in the humanities in general. In 1996 *PMLA* devoted a guest column to "Four Views on the Place of the Personal in Scholarship." Although the four scholars whose views are presented do not agree on every point, all of them agree that the personal belongs in scholarship. In the lead article, "Against Subjectivity," Michael Bérubé writes that he "would not go so far as to imagine that personal narratives constitute some kind of generic violation of scholarship in the human sciences: as long as the scholarship in question concerns humans and is written by humans, readers should at least entertain the possibility that nothing human should be alien to it" (1065). Since my dissertation was about a human experience I happen to share, personal narratives should, according to Bérubé's argument, be permissible.

Bérubé also reasons that using the personal can, paradoxically, contribute to objectivity. Scholars can be more aware of their own biases when they confront their relationship to their topic. As Bérubé explains, "unless scholars try to understand how, historically, we humans have construed the world we half see and half create, they will lapse into the worst form of subjectivism—projecting their own interpretive idiosyncrasies onto their research while blithely believing that they've finally grasped the object as in itself it really is" (1066). I surely found this to be the case. The personal narratives were the most difficult part of my dissertation to write because until I set out to do this writing, I had not spent much time thinking about my deafness as an object or about how deafness shaped the way I experienced and viewed the world.

For the first time, through my personal narrative, I acknowledged the impact being deaf had on my life in general and on my education in particular. I had wanted to think that because I had done so well in school (gotten all the way to writing a doctoral dissertation!) that being deaf was just there, part of me, like having brown eyes. However, while writing my dissertation I had to acknowledge that my mainstreamed education had many negative aspects as well as positive. I ended the process much less sure of what I had gotten out of my education because for the first time I had to confront how much I had missed. I even came to believe that there was a strong possibility, even a probability, that I was in graduate school in the first place because academics let me interact more with books than with people. These were painful considerations, inducing severe writer's block. I did not want to know these things, yet I had to think about them to be able to write about them.

The pain of writing the personal narrative sections, however, paid off in the rest of my dissertation. Because my biases were clearer to myself, I was able to be more balanced in my approach. One of the big differences between the original seminar paper and my dissertation is that the dissertation does a better job of acknowledging the difficulties deaf students face in learning English. The original seminar paper suggested that if only hearing culture provided the right opportunities, deaf children would be able to learn English just like hearing children. Although I still believe that changes can go a long way to making it easier, I also now believe that the difficulties will not go away even in ideal conditions. I needed to explore how my experiences contributed to my beliefs before I could see that.

If the goal of a dissertation is to produce the best piece of original scholarship a student is capable of, in a manner appropriate to one's field, then personal narrative should not only be acceptable but desirable. Allowing graduate students the full range of written expression should be especially important to rhetoricians who understand the importance of ethos and who should not exclude a whole mode of communication, especially a mode that enables a writer to both establish and question the authority of her experience. I am not a disinterested observer; why should I pretend to be? It is a matter of academic honesty.

Chapter Eleven

Dissertating in a Digital Age
The Future of Composition Scholarship

Janice R. Walker and Joseph M. Moxley

At the 2001 Conference on Electronic Theses and Dissertations (ETDs), Joe shared with Simon Pockley his desire to develop a database of exemplary and innovative ETDs.[1] Pockley warned, "Beware! Don't do it! You're creating a monster!" and then explained how his dissertation, "The Flight of Ducks" (1995), which was also Australia's first ETD, has been accessed by over one million different computers, with over 200 million distinct hits[2] (Pockley 1995, 2001). Pockley corresponds with dozens of new readers interested in his dissertation's subject—a multimedia presentation and critical examination of his father's writings and photographs from Australia—and his experience writing Australia's first ETD. Although his work was a labor of love, it has become, because of its volume, a "monster" that has extended his research beyond the dissertation's publication in 1995. "The monster," he says,

> lies within the interactive aspect of networked communities. If you open yourself up to discussion or comment or hate mail or whatever, you have to appreciate the sheer size of the world out there. It's full of people who are interested and some people will respond. Trouble is, they keep on responding—month after month year after year [sic]. 'The Flight of Ducks' has been on-line now since 1995. Although the response looks like it's leveling off, it's getting more thoughtful. I'm pretty stretched for time these days and it takes time and effort to reply. I guess I could ignore these people but they are interesting and compelling and they represent a kind of constituent community of interest. A community of interest that is largely of my own making—I can't ignore them. Besides, I like the way that our contacts often turn towards actually meeting. I like meeting them, I like having dinner with them, I like the uncertainty of the relationship that is constantly being challenged or renewed. (Pockley 2001)

Conversations Pockley has had with readers are archived online.[3] They range from insightful queries about his work to entirely off-the-wall comments. For example, while some readers request information about particular aboriginal tribes, respond to themes and issues raised by his work, or reflect on his presentation, others seek weird advice, such as the Mexican shrimp farmer who wanted to know how to make ducks fly away so they won't eat his shrimp. Nevertheless, Pockley's ETD broke new ground with the potential to shift dissertators and their advisors from talking about the dissertation as being, ideally, *like* a social conversation to examining what happens when a dissertation *is* a social conversation.

In addition to writing Australia's first ETD, Pockley also fought a bitter censorship battle with his University's Research Ethics Committee. Displeased with his depiction of aboriginal people—or, rather, worried about how these images might be used beyond *Flight of the Ducks*—the committee attempted to ban and regulate his work. Specifically, the committee was concerned that the digitized images he included would be torn from their context and bastardized (a problem that he seeks to confront, contextualize, and debate rather than eliminate by taking his dissertation off-line). Because of this ongoing censorship battle, Pockley's work is still not archived at the university where he earned his PhD; however, it has been hosted at other servers around the world, including the National Library of Australia, Project Xanadu, and the University of Michigan.

Despite his difficulties with his home university, Pockley's story is inspiring. He created a dissertation that is widely read, one that has ignited discussion across the globe. Yet in many respects, Pockley's online dissertation isn't exemplary at all. The format is sometimes difficult to read, difficult to print, and not necessarily hypertextual. That is, while Pockley includes digitized images, animated graphics, and hypertextual links, there is nothing in the dissertation itself that couldn't have been presented in traditional print format. What does make this work unique is the ongoing conversation that surrounds it, conversation that is encouraged by its publication online.

Keith Dorwick's (1996–1998) dissertation project at the University of Illinois at Chicago, "Building the Virtual Department: A Case Study of Online Teaching and Research," uses frames, annoying pop-up windows,[4] and, like Pockley, often-confusing navigational cues to present textual information that would have been easier to read in a traditional print format. However, Dorwick also includes software for both synchronous (i.e., real-time) and asynchronous communication, along with Web-based forms as part of his dissertation project, so that his dissertation continues to grow as readers' responses are incorporated into the project. The conversations allowed by the software are an integral part of Dorwick's project—in some respects, the conversation *is* the project. So, while the metadiscussion Dorwick presents could easily have been presented in a more traditional format (i.e., print), the software not only requires electronic publication; it requires publication online.

Ed Fox (Fox, MacMillan, Eaton 1999), director of the Networked Digital Library of Theses and Dissertations at Virginia Tech, notes there are two types of ETDs: one that is "prepared by the (student) author . . . using some electronic tools" (e.g., word processors) and submitted in electronic form, and those created by university or service staff (e.g., UMI) by "scanning in the pages of a paper thesis or dissertation." Obviously, neither of these two types requires electronic publication per se. And for the most part, ETDs published at the Networked Digital Library are mired in tradition. Nonetheless, the potential of electronic production and publication is provocative, allowing for collaborative work, innovations in format and content, and wider dissemination of important graduate research.

Traditionally, of course, the dissertation has been considered the first work of original research by a candidate, the successful completion of which allows access to the profession. But this view elides the true collaborative nature of the dissertation, as candidates work closely with their committees to develop their projects and bring them to fruition. How would our conception of the dissertation change if it were to include not only the product of the student's research but the process as well? That is, what if readers could trace the project from inception to publication and, perhaps, even extend the research by adding comments of their own? Would it make a difference if the conversations with committee members were incorporated, perhaps hypertextually, into the dissertation itself? What if the defense were held online as well, like Dene Grigar's (Grigar and Barber 1997) online dissertation defense at Lingua MOO, or by incorporating audio and/or video files, asynchronous discussions (e.g., email discussion), or electronic marginalia into the work itself?

New media scholarship makes it possible to include many voices, in ways that may challenge our conception of authorship entirely. Of course, merely including other voices doesn't necessarily pose such a challenge, but experimentation with new forms may challenge us in other ways. Paulette Robinson, as a student at Towson University, for example, completed her dissertation on student use of Web-based conferencing (2000), replete with Shockwave Flash movies (well designed and conceived, but annoying after the first flush), student comments in both text and streaming audio, and a hypernews forum so well password-protected that interested readers cannot even access it. Her use of animated menus, image maps, and color-coded indexes to organize her work results in a dissertation that is game-like but frustrating because of its lack of traditional cues. As Robinson (2001) herself asks:

> What does it look like to think spatial in a network of connections? What would the conventions look like? Or, [do] there have to be conventions? How much cognitive bridging or conceptual mapping does the reader need to feel familiar and not confused or frustrated? Does the reader build comfort by revisiting the piece and begin to gain familiarity through visitations? How do we build new notational systems?

> My design was not a game. It is experimentation with how to use the Web in a postmodern and more spatial way. It is my belief that the Web offers an opportunity to move away from a linear book presentation mode and incorporate other forms of processing information.

Part of the problem with dissertations such as Robinson's, which push the margins—literally—beyond the one-inch margins allowed by paper to the (more or less) limitless margins allowed in cyberspace, is that few of us are really comfortable reading these works. Casual readers may enjoy the sense of play and discovery, but serious readers may be frustrated by the limitations imposed on us by our training in linear forms. And yet, without such experimentation, how can we fulfill the needs of future readers, readers for whom traditional linear forms are quickly becoming archaic?

In her plenary address to the Research Network Forum at the 2001 Conference on College Composition and Communication, Janice argued that

> We don't yet know how to read and write in a digital age, let alone how to teach our students. In many ways, our students are teaching us. However, as long as our assessment practices (for both students *and* faculty) continue to privilege the status quo (requiring students to pass large-scale testing applications that require handwritten essays, or giving more weight to single-authored, print publications in faculty tenure reviews, for example), and as long as our graduate programs continue to place computers and writing work on the margins of what we do, then our classrooms will remain in danger of becoming as anachronistic as teaching our students to make their own quill pens. (Walker 2001)

Whether we like it or not, computers and the World Wide Web have forever changed the landscape of reading, writing, and research. Our students have been raised with a remote control in one hand and a computer mouse in the other; failing to allow for serious scholarship that reflects the changes in literacy practices that new and emerging technologies foster (or foist upon us) won't make these changes go away. Instead, what we will be left with is trying to figure out what happened while we weren't looking—a bit like teaching our students how to make their own paper and ink in a world gone digital. One change that we need to heed is that wrought in citation formats by the Internet: Although many still debate how to cite electronic formats in print documents, only *The Columbia Guide to Online Style* (Walker and Taylor 1998) offers alternative formats for citing print and electronic sources in electronic documents. Since documentation of such sources is an important component of graduate research, academics need to pay attention to these discussions.

Within the field of composition, Christine Boese's dissertation from Rensselaer Polytechnic Institute—"The Ballad of the Internet Nutball: Chaining Rhetorical Visions from the Margins of the Margins to the Mainstream in the Xenaverse" (1998–2000)—provides another example of the new media dissertation and its challenges. With its intricate navigation,[5] use of sound files, interactive features (including a forum and a survey), and self-generating nature, "Ballad" is not only a format-checker's worst nightmare, it also raises the question of what constitutes fair use of copyrighted materials. Boese claims her use of photos, sound, and video clips of Xena, the Warrior Princess, copyrighted by MCA/Universal Studies, falls under the provisions of academic fair use. The doctrine of fair use, however, is already under attack, and rules as to how to extend this doctrine's provisions to new media scholarship—especially when that scholarship is published freely online—have yet to be determined. Whose job will it be to determine the guidelines for use of copyrighted material in ETDs? Will the same guidelines we follow for more traditional theses and dissertations apply when our libraries are publishing the works on their Web servers, making them easily searchable and accessible from anywhere in the world?

Thanks to the Networked Digital Library of Theses and Dissertations, an emerging worldwide digital library of ETDs, graduate students can realistically expect their research to attract thousands, even millions, of readers. Virginia Tech's digital collection (where ETDs have been required for graduation since 1997) boasted 221,679 requests for ETDs in PDF format in its first full year, 1997–1998; 481,038 in 1998–1999; 578,152 in 1999–2000; and a whopping 2,173,420 in 2000–2001 (Networked Digital Library 2001). Since its creation in 1996 with support from FIPSE, the Networked Digital Library has emerged as a world leader in electronic publication of graduate theses and dissertations. Although young, the library includes over 106 member institutions and research universities. Another sixty of the universities that attended the Network Digital Library conference in March 2001 were not yet members but were interested in joining and clamoring for training materials.

American universities for the most part, however, have been slow to institutionalize ETD initiatives. All but a small handful of universities who have joined the Networked Digital Library are mired in pilot projects, unsure about which authoring platforms to support, lacking resources or expertise to develop training materials, and often facing resistance from both graduate faculty and graduate students. Currently, only five American universities require ETDs: Virginia Tech, West Virginia University, East Tennessee State University, the University of North Texas, and the University of Texas at Austin. In contrast, Australia, France, and Germany have developed national models for organizing ETDs and are at various stages of implementing mandatory ETD policies at the national level to guide and standardize the development of local ETD initiatives.

The French Ministry of Education and Research, for example, has established a national scheme for archiving and encoding metadata, and the Minister of Education has "published a public circulaire [i.e., a public letter] addressed to the president of every university and graduate school announcing his wish to develop ETDs at a national level" (Bouletreau 2001). Tony Cargnelutti (2001) reports Australia has created the Australian Digital Theses Program, a national collaborative model originally developed by seven leading Australian universities which now coordinates ETDs for 43.5 percent of Australia's universities. And in 1997, according to Susanne Dobratz (2001), "the German Conference on University Rectors (Hochschulrektorenkonferenz) placed a statement that said universities should allow the electronic publication of dissertations as one of the possibilities to fulfill the publication requirements."

In some ways, American universities are wise to proceed with caution. The Network Digital Library initiative is in its infancy, and those involved are still in the process of developing metatagging standards, archival standards, and protocols for publication and searching. Archivists are justifiably concerned that today's Macromedia Flash or Real Media or Windows Media dissertation may not be viewable in five or ten years. However, most librarians don't see this as a problem. What *is* a problem is a lack of standards.

University Microforms International (UMI) currently makes American doctoral research available worldwide—for a fee. For the most part, UMI has relied on paper copies, bound or unbound. More recently, however, UMI has made doctoral dissertations available electronically, using a bitmap scan which is usually inferior in quality and functionality to an author-produced ETD. The bitmapped image cannot be indexed and searched or analyzed, it doesn't contain functioning links, and it does not and cannot include audio or video files. In other words, the UMI electronic version of the dissertation is really no more than a photographic image of a print dissertation. While this is a step toward making graduate scholarship more accessible, UMI's fee structure ensures that this service will be available only to those who are willing and able to pay for it. One goal of the Networked Digital Library, on the other hand, is to make work freely available worldwide. It also encourages submission of masters' theses, unlike UMI which focuses mainly on PhD work.

In addition to the copyright concerns mentioned earlier, ETDs pose additional problems for graduate studies departments and libraries, including problems with archiving and academic publishing. What parameters, if any, should be imposed on graduate student work in new media? For example, should graduate students be limited to a certain number of bytes? Should they be required to submit ETDs only in certain formats—Word or Word Perfect documents; print document format (PDF); HTML, XML, DTML, or some other variation of markup language? What format should be used for multimedia files—graphics, audio, video? Currently, there isn't even agreement on standards for publishing Web pages—files that may appear fine in Microsoft's Internet Explorer browser may appear quite different (if, indeed, they appear at all) when viewed in Netscape Communicator. How do we balance the need for flexibility in the face of extraordinary changes in the technologies of writing and research with the need for standards by which to judge the work's suitability? Following the model of the German universities, the graduate dissertation has traditionally proven a student's readiness to enter the profession. Perhaps it's time to rethink the purpose of graduate scholarship, especially as this work becomes readily and freely available online, a resource for future researchers and, conceivably, an ongoing or collaborative work for both authors and their readers.

At any rate, this is the part of the scholarly discussion where compositionists are sorely needed, particularly those with expertise in computers and composition. Presently, most ETD enthusiasts are found in engineering colleges or university libraries, while compositionists—as researchers or writers—have been remarkably silent. In our opinion, graduate students and their mentors in composition are especially well qualified to serve as leaders in the ETD movement. For decades, compositionists have argued that our colleagues outside of composition need to hear about process pedagogies, about principles of visual rhetoric, about ways to revise and collaborate facilitated by online protocols. ETDs can provide such a forum. We can help faculty across disciplines reevaluate the goals of graduate theses and dissertations. We can help faculty and students better understand related intellectual property issues, hopefully overcoming the current tendency for nearly half of the students who write ETDs to restrict access to their home campuses. We can develop courses and training materials—extending the work of writing-across-the-curriculum (WAC) advocates beyond the first-year composition course to graduate programs. And we can explore how new and emerging technologies can be used to advance mentoring. Presently, half of the students who complete their coursework across disciplines fail to complete their dissertations (Baird 1990; Bowen and Rudenstine1992; Smith 2000).

Compositionists can also lend their expertise to developing technologies for writing, research, and collaboration. For example, as part of the Computers and Writing Conference hosted by Texas Woman's University in May 2000, Janice founded and coordinated the first Graduate Research Network (GRN), a forum for "graduate students, adjuncts, and recent graduates to discuss research projects and works-in-progress of interest to those working with Computers and Writing with experienced researchers, editors, and peers" (Graduate Research Network 2002). The GRN is now in its third year and growing, including an online forum in addition to the annual preconference workshop at the Computers and Writing Conference. What if the GRN were to join forces with the Networked Digital Library, fostering collaboration and development of new media scholarship that can stand as a model for our own discipline—and perhaps for others?

We need to consider how an up-to-date, worldwide, digital library of theses and dissertations would affect interdisciplinary research. Think about it for a moment: If, in a heartbeat, a student could download timely reviews of literature and see how others were making meaning, defending methodologies, and using streaming multimedia, while, with another click, the student could discuss completed dissertations or new ideas with other researchers—if a student could do all this, would the face of graduate research change? To many, the current dissertation project is little more than a hoop—the only good dissertation is, after all, a done dissertation. While many newly minted PhDs hope to turn their dissertation projects into their first published monographs, the works generally require complete rewriting—even rethinking—before they are suitable for publication to a wider audience, tied as they are to "school" formats. What would happen if PhD candidates wrote for real audiences instead of writing only for their committees?

Imagine, for example, students developing an online portfolio at the beginning of their career, then using this online space to maintain an annotated bibliography, links to documents written during coursework, to online syllabi of coursework taken, and to archives of online conversations. Rather than having a graduate student receive criticism from one professor at a time, he or she could post the work to a campus network and provide whatever document security he or she wished; then the faculty could access the work and post comments, criticisms, and suggestions. Imagine graduate students at universities throughout the world having access not only to completed dissertation projects but to works in progress. Imagine dissertations being written for real audiences—even lay audiences.

Imagine, too, as graduate students and graduate faculty become comfortable with new writing and researching tools, online dissertations that incorporate animation, three-dimensional modeling, multimedia, and ongoing conversations, dissertations that cross space and time, that grow and change even years after the author has been awarded his or her degree—in short, imagine a dissertation that is more than just a ticket to the profession but that is a continuing contribution to the body of knowledge in a discipline, a work that can grow along with the career of its author. New media scholarship not only attracts new readers; today's multimedia dissertations can serve as models for a new genre of scholarship that future students may emulate (Fox, McMillan, and Eaton 1999), as innovative researchers and scholars challenge conventions.

Clearly, new technologies are transforming our research, teaching, and writing processes. They are also threatening our cherished conventions, such as the five-chapter dissertation with one-inch margins. Understandably, many faculty and university leaders are unsure how to use software tools to mentor students, format documents, or collaborate online, not to mention are unaware of what benefits, if any, might accrue. As Kenneth Green's yearly survey of campus technology trends has demonstrated, faculty are not always willing to use new technologies: "I think it's fair to say that many faculty members have ceded to their students the whole issue of technology skills" (qtd. in Olsen, 1999). Regardless, fields other than composition—especially in the hard sciences—are already leading the way as the high cost of publishing forces many journals in engineering and the sciences to move online. It's time for compositionists to catch up. Our definitions of literacy, our ways of constructing and disseminating meaning, have dramatically changed, and we must transform our universities if we hope to remain relevant. Anything less is academic myopia.

End Notes

1. Simon Pockley and Joe Moxley are among those working with colleagues at the Australian Digital Theses Project; Humboldt-University Berlin; ISTEC: Ibero-American Science Technology Education Consortium; National Library of Portugal; VIDYANIDHI: Digital Library of Indian Electronic Theses; Virginia Tech; Universidad de Chile; Université de Lyon; and Université de Montreal to create an online resource of best ETD practices published by UNESCO. See UNESCO (2001) (http://etdguide.org) for more information.

2. Web server statistics for "Flight of the Ducks" are as follows. Successful requests: 1,128,357. Average successful requests per day: 2,265. Successful requests for pages: 533,057. Average successful requests for pages per day: 1,070. Redirected requests: 81. Data transferred: 9,256 Gbytes. Average data transferred per day: 19,032 Mbytes.

3. See http://www.acmi.net.au/FOD/FOD0989.html and http://www.acmi.net.au/FOD/FOD0882.html, for example.

4. Not all pop-up windows are annoying (though some people are annoyed by all of them). The windows that Dorwick uses, however, pop up whenever the mouse moves over text on the page. Thus, unless one is particularly careful, the windows will continue to pop up as the user tries to move the mouse pointer back to the desired position on the page.

5. Boese (1998–2000) notes in her dissertation:

> This dissertation is a hypertextual performance in nonlinear form. It is both expressive and paradigmatic, descriptive and analytical, as it seeks the cultural logic of an electronically linked society in cyberspace: The Xenaverse. As such it exists on the Web and on CD-ROM. This presentation consists of webbed nodes of hypertext rather than chapters, both reflecting and contributing to the webbed electronic environment in which the Xenaverse exists.

In other words, Boese's text is itself an enactment of changing literacy practices. As such, it plays freely with navigational features in an attempt to model possibilities. The table of contents opens in a pop-up window, with text displayed in the main window; however, links within the text also appear in the main window, so that the reader may lose track of which nodes have been read and which haven't.

Chapter Twelve

Why Write a Dissertation?

Marsha Lee Holmes

"All you have to do is finish; it doesn't matter how good it is."
"The job market is so tight, my advice is 'Publish, publish, publish.'"
"He's obviously the best candidate; he has a book contract."
"Good grief—it's just a dissertation!"

At my alma mater, two myths of a dissertation's purpose send mixed messages to graduate students in composition and rhetoric. One myth says that the best dissertation is a done dissertation (no matter how good it is) while the other insists that the best dissertation is a published dissertation (no matter what good it does). In such a setting doctoral students write to "get it done" or "to get it published"—and since publication depends on completion, either myth indicates that getting it done is more important than what gets done. The material reality of the dissertation scene reinforces the "get it done" mentality as teaching assistantships and student loans become threatened and threatening the longer it takes to finish. For instance, a teaching assistant in my doctoral program can anticipate contract renewal for four years and then pray for a fifth during which they had better "get it done." Although many veteran scholars find it difficult to write a solid book-length draft in one year, doctoral candidates find that their finances depend on it. While struggling to get it done, they also hear they had better get it published—their future in higher education depends on it.

Two pieces of advice for selecting members of doctoral committees circulate through my graduate institution's English department that, not coincidentally, bolster these two myths about a dissertation's purpose. On one hand, graduate students are advised to choose the most humane people they know to increase their chances of getting the dissertation done quickly and sanely. On the other, students are urged to persuade the most prominent scholars available to join their committee to strengthen their chances for publication. My own approach to committee selection was to try to resist both the get-it-done and get-it-published forces, to choose people I'd found to be intelligent, insightful, good-humored, and trustworthy, who helped educate students and colleagues both in and out of the classroom.

Writing about the experience of working with this committee and writing that dissertation has turned out be more complex and messy than I'd anticipated when I agreed to contribute a chapter to *The Dissertation and the Discipline*. Slowly I've begun to realize that this confusion was caused by the same problems I'd faced in the dissertation: Despite my best efforts, my purposes for writing were contradictory, and my relationship to readers unclear. The recurrence of these difficulties in my postdoctoral scholarship has stung all the more because it undermines the commitment central to both my dissertation and this essay—to exchange performance in writing for genuine acts of learning. In my dissertation I examined how contemporary rhetoric perpetuates a classical notion of epideictic discourse as ceremonial—composed for the moment, seeking praise from readers for its mastery, with no consciousness of affecting the future. A performance of form. So that composition students might occasion less ceremonial and more communicative discourse in school, I'd argued for re-visioning purpose in first-year composition and rebalancing power between student writers and teacher readers. For this chapter I'd aimed to apply these arguments to the dissertation itself, arguing that it too needs transforming into more genuine communication and meaningful learning. Yet the writing journal I've kept when I could write nothing else makes clear that I myself didn't resolve the questions of purpose and audience in my dissertation and have had trouble resolving them in this first occasion to write after receiving my doctorate.

I don't believe this problem is particular to me. Think of it: At one end of a hall we find composition and rhetoric doctoral students urging undergraduate composition students to write beyond the purpose of a grade, to imagine audiences beyond the teacher. At the other end, we find those same doctoral students revising dissertations that they hope will satisfy committee members just enough for a passing grade or acquisition editors more than enough for a contract. While creating occasions for students to write genuinely, as their composition and rhetoric professors have taught them to do, these graduate writers struggle with their own reasons for writing, sensing a great disparity between what they are doing and what it will accomplish. Instead of applying the very best of what's to be learned in their discipline—connections between word and world, process and product, means and end—they abandon what they've learned in this, the final act of student writing. In a discipline dedicated to transforming dichotomies, how can this be?

In order for me to answer that question with integrity, I have had to create an essay that is far more personal than, frankly, I had anticipated or wanted. It speaks directly about the actual people and place that shaped my dissertation experience—people I love and respect in a department for which I'm deeply grateful. Yet, I assert, we fashioned an unnecessarily flawed educational experience that, counter to the best of teaching in composition and rhetoric, not only valued ends over means but also sent contradictory messages about what the ends should be: Just get it done; good grief, it's only a dissertation! Get it published; it's your academic career on the line.

I don't remember that my committee and I ever discussed the purpose of writing a dissertation, and if we assumed agreement about purpose, we were wrong. I only had departmental myths to go on and hunches about which myth each committee member valued. For instance, as we chatted at a departmental social event, one member suggested that the merits of "getting it published" were self-evident. "That's the only reason I can think of for writing one," she shrugged. A fellow student offered clues about another committee member who had informed her that she'd better write a publishable dissertation if she wanted a job. Did that advice apply to me as well? If yes, why hadn't he told me the same thing? A third committee member talked in such flatly practical terms that the only message I inferred was "get it done." Her disparaging description of a dissertation's rhetorical situation—a student arguing to her teachers in order to gain their approval—sounded not only forthright and accurate but consonant with the central concern of my dissertation, an examination of the ceremonial rhetoric pervading students' writing for school. The chair of my committee advised me (in line with the best of contemporary composition studies) to write first for my own understanding, but with no further discussion of purpose beyond self-understanding. A year into the writing, she began to tailor her revision advice toward helping me gain committee members' approval. She was helping me meet the "get-it-done" goal even though that myth of purpose didn't square with the way she had taught me to teach writing.

My oral defense highlights the problem of unclear, unexamined purpose. My chair and I thought that I would talk about further evidence for and implications of my argument while the committee would suggest ways to continue developing this research. We also would discuss connections between this study and my future teaching and writing. We didn't anticipate a traditional, combative defense but instead a dynamic link from doctoral to postdoctoral work.

One member was unable to attend, having moved to another university, and I was never made aware of the comments and questions she had mailed for inclusion in the defense. Another member arrived ready to sign off with approval. Since she had another meeting an hour later, she joked that my defense would be short, sweet, and (to my disappointment) "ceremonial." The third member announced two major reservations about approving the dissertation.

He outlined his concerns and the ensuing discussion felt like a battle, him against my chair and me, with the other member uncertain about which side to join. As the battle wound down, the "ceremonial" member casually but perkily mentioned that I had the "makings of a book on my hands." After several beats, my chair murmured, "Oh . . . um . . . yes." The resisting reader sat silently. Where, I thought, did that "get it published" comment come from? It was the first time anyone had mentioned publication, and though I liked my dissertation, I honestly didn't hear a book in it. Her comment sounded token-like and unconvincing. I left the defense, revised the third chapter, wrote a preface, and graduated three weeks later.

I had gotten it done, but I was not finished with the "get it published" myth. One member was willing to update letters of reference only if the publishing record had changed. The resistant member fell back into silence, not acknowledging news of my accepting a tenure-track position. My committee chair praised another former student for publishing a dissertation but did not inquire about my own scholarship, even about a project to which she knew we were both contributing. I risk sounding petty, insecure, or, even worse, ungrateful. Nevertheless, I take that chance to illustrate the extent to which a lack of clear, shared purpose influences us long after the dissertation itself is done.

I must, of course, revisit my own sense of purpose—a sense, I've discovered, that shifted during the eighteen months in which I wrote my dissertation. When I began writing, I fantasized about winning the university's "best dissertation award," and so I imagined readers from the prize's multidisciplinary committee of scholars with varying opinions and knowledge of English studies. My dream for this award appears competitive, yet I was not driven only to win. I was driven to communicate, to persuade. I wanted my dissertation to communicate with as many people as possible. I imagined that winning this award would mean I'd achieved that.

The purpose shifted when I began receiving committee members' responses to drafts and so began to focus on the committee as my intended readers. In fact, I spent the next couple of months trying to believe that I would communicate my argument to four professors in the English department. They were, I told myself, the most real(istic) group of intended readers I could address. But this revised rhetorical triangle was more neat than accurate. Two of these committee-member readers were the professors who had led me to virtually everything I'd learned about rhetoric and composition. They each had been instrumental in helping me discover and articulate the essence of my dissertation's argument. So, I sensed I had little opportunity to persuade them of anything: I would be preaching to the choir. Furthermore, these two teachers didn't act like intended readers. The chair worked as a mentor, nurturing my thinking, writing, and learning throughout the dissertation experience. The other composition and rhetoric specialist and I had a similar relationship. In lengthy, long distance telephone conversations, she helped me figure out how to keep writing in this increasingly frustrating rhetorical situation even though, I sensed, she perceived the dissertation as an academic exercise not worth a great deal of my sweat. With insight and intelligence, both of these teachers encouraged and commiserated. I was fortunate to have their faithful support, but I never believed they were my intended readers, and they never assumed that role. As for the two other committee members, rhetoric was ancillary to their literary scholarship and teaching. It seemed unlikely that they would choose to read a (my) book-length study of epideictic discourse, so I could not, then, imagine them as intended readers either, especially if the dissertation aimed toward publication. They did, of course, influence my writing, but in a way that prompted me to feel like my first-year composition students who tried to do what they thought I wanted in order to get the grade they wanted. After receiving members' comments on each draft, my chair and I discussed revisions based primarily on what would satisfy them enough to approve the dissertation, not to convince them of its argument. I started yearning to finish this writing as soon as possible, though I knew that just getting it done pushed me dangerously close to writing a text antithetical to my dissertation's aims: a text that performed rather than persuaded; a text that sought praise rather than deliberation.

I don't know why I did not continue my search for a believable group of intended readers. About a year into the process, I began telling myself that my dissertation wasn't going to be award-winning quality. In other words, I could not write well enough. Or, I would say, I was too closure-oriented to take the necessary additional year to achieve that quality. In other words, I could write well enough, but I wouldn't construct a plan allowing me to do so. I still wonder: What if my belief in communicating had held stronger?

I wonder too if the battle that took place at my oral defense suggests that my desire to communicate wasn't completely unfulfilled. Although the resisting reader's dissension seemed poorly timed, it did provoke what seemed to be genuine deliberation. When he challenged my argument's reliance on the war eulogy and claimed that a eulogy occasioned by the death of a child would be a fairer test, he caught the attention of the member who had been ready to praise and go. The three of us participated in an earnest discussion of these two distinctly different eulogistic occasions and their implications for my conclusions about contemporary epideictic theory and practice. I listened to their arguments; they mulled over my responses. During this portion of the defense, I remember having mixed feelings: exhilaration that part of my argument was actually being considered, frustration that its deliberation had not come sooner (or later), anxiety about the life-changing consequences of not satisfying my committee's requirements, heart sickness that the final revisions would illustrate my weakness in adhering to my own argument about school writing. But as I revised, I remembered that one evanescent moment in which two readers and I engaged in influencing one another's thinking. I had not entirely lost my goal to learn and to persuade.

Yet, as I said at the start of this chapter, writing this essay about my dissertation has not been easy; that one moment from my dissertation defense didn't forever restore the belief that my writing can be purposeful, that my words can persuade. I've struggled for my voice in this chapter by trying to sound knowledgeable rather than trying to gain knowledge. I also fell into the myth of "get it published" since this publication could earn me credibility at my doctoral alma mater and in my tenure-track position. The pressure to finish (read: get it published) overwhelmed me until the urge to learn finally won out. I decided to write to figure out what had happened with both this essay and my dissertation. Frankly, I no longer cared whether anyone else would read it, but I did care deeply about my own survival and livelihood as a teacher-scholar—as a person willing and able to think through an issue of importance to herself. It may sound like I simply needed to close my eyes and write, taking Peter Elbow's (1987) sound advice for ignoring audience. And I did do that, though there was something more fundamental I had to do: I had to listen to my own dissertation's argument about impoverished ceremonial discourse, let that argument persuade me, stop seeking the praise of this collection's editors, stop performing a form. Only then could I find intended readers to persuade.

Of all places, this listening and learning needs to thrive in dissertations, a place for the best fruits of composition-rhetoric's educational labor. Nobody involved in my dissertation would have wished anything less. But in order to assure this outcome, graduate students and faculty need to address questions such as these: What are the similarities and differences between the chair's role and the roles of other committee members? Does the standard committee need restructuring? How can committee members develop beyond the position of judge? How do departments perpetuate myths about dissertations and how can students and faculty reshape those myths through specific approaches to dissertation writing and advising? How can we use the dissertation to reconceive what academic discourse is—and can be?

So why did I write a dissertation? To explore a topic at the core of my teaching and scholarship; to develop and articulate a philosophy of composition teaching; to transform the information of doctoral seminars and comprehensive exams into knowledge. These lessons—foundational, dynamic, generative—I will rethink, reshape, and rearticulate throughout my career, in many ways with many people. How do other teacher-scholars in composition and rhetoric studies see it, though? Are such lessons enough to earn one a PhD? And what about the idea that one's future depends not only on getting it done but also on getting it published? Let's admit it: Publish-or-perish is a reality.

But is it the only reality? When I interviewed for the university position that I currently hold, the search committee sought assurances that my commitment to the field of composition and rhetoric was genuine (not a tenure-track foot in the door), and they dedicated most of my campus visit to getting to know me as a teacher. What I learned through writing my dissertation served me well during that visit, as it continues to nourish my teaching and scholarship—and my advising of graduate students—today. Mine was a dissertation worth doing, not one done just to be done. It was a dissertation worth doing, whether published or not (it's not).

Chapter Thirteen

"You Both Looked the Same to Me"
Collaboration as Subversion

Amy Goodburn and Carrie Shively Leverenz

This story is about collaboration and its role in preparing graduate students in rhetoric and composition to be professionals. It is our story of how we came to collaborate in the dissertation stage and, simultaneously, in our searches for tenure-track jobs and (only a little later) in our scholarly activities. In particular, this story is about the complications of collaborating within academic institutions—as graduate students and then as untenured faculty—given the intractable values associated with those institutions, most obviously, the privileging of individual accomplishment and the valorization of competition resulting in a zero-sum game of academic success. Although the dominance of social constructionist theories of knowledge-production that suffused our graduate training in the early 1990s led us to view collaboration as an obvious and necessary good, our subsequent experiences suggest that the revolution has not moved very far out of our old neighborhood. We want to go beyond an idyllic portrayal of collaboration in graduate programs to consider how collaborative practices shape professional identities and the consequences of these identities when graduate students move into other departmental cultures. Ultimately, we argue that the choice to collaborate within an institution that inhibits or devalues such collaboration must be made in full awareness of the risks as well as the potential benefits.

While the heyday of research and theorizing about social constructionism now appears to be over, one lasting benefit of that work was its uncovering of the deeply rooted historical and philosophical resistance to collaboration. Kurt Spellmeyer (1998) describes the culture of English departments as highly stratified and competitive bureaucracies where "Learning how to be an English studies professional requires the beginner to emulate those who have 'made it' . . . from the standpoint of the individual career" (169). Scholars such as Patricia A. Sullivan (1994) and Elizabeth Ervin and Dana L. Fox (1994) have illuminated how this construct of the independent scholar devalues collaborative activity. In *Lifting a Ton of Feathers* Paula J. Caplan (1995) lists as one myth about academia that "people's search for knowledge is done cooperatively and not competitively, and that this cooperation is rewarded" (53). The culture itself, then, helps account for the difficulty in providing spaces for collaborative work despite the calls for its general value.

The question of how to prepare graduate students for academic jobs has received a great deal of attention recently, primarily because of the dismal job market for English PhDs.[1] Although graduate students with concentrations in rhetoric and composition continue to fare better than their counterparts, many of the available jobs include heavy administrative responsibilities or high teaching loads. In "Present Perfect and Future Imperfect," Scott L. Miller, Brenda Jo Brueggemann, Bennis Blue, and Deneen M. Shepherd (1997) report the results of a national 1993 survey of graduate students in rhetoric and composition. An important finding is that while more than 80 percent of the graduate students surveyed said they were satisfied or very satisfied with their graduate programs, most also admitted that they knew little about what their futures would look like. These researchers argue that "programs need to be (more) accountable for the 'future perfect tense' of graduate students" (400), noting that "the real question is how programs can enact both needs—to be honest and overt about professional realities and to create and maintain stimulating, enriching, and welcoming places in which new scholars can develop" (399).

Much of the recent attention on professionalizing graduate students in rhetoric and composition has focused on preparing them for administrative responsibilities (Pemberton 1993; Long, Holberg, and Taylor 1996)—one area where, because of the complexity of the task, collaboration is encouraged, even required. (A double issue of the journal *Writing Program Administration* was devoted to the subject of collaborative writing program administration.) Such collaboration is often portrayed as particularly beneficial to graduate students in developing collegiality, experience in decision making, and an analysis of the complex relationship between writing programs and institutional cultures (see, for instance, Anson and Rutz 1998). Collaborative administrative work is not without its difficulties, however, in part because it remains within an institution where power is still organized in a strict hierarchy. Eileen Schell (1998a) points out that "the scholarship on collaborative writing program administration . . . has, for the most part, remained strangely silent about the tensions and conflicts that accompany collaborative leadership efforts, often painting collaborative administration as a utopian or progressive, non-hierarchical practice" (77). Few scholars address the professional reality of moving from a highly collaborative graduate program to take a job in a more traditional English department that is suspicious of collaborative work.

Past

Our experiences with collaboration began fairly early in our graduate careers, both formal and informal structures shaping our understanding of collaborative practices in graduate school and in academic work in general. Perhaps it's important to mention that we were first colleagues, then friends, that it was our collaborative work in a number of different forums that led to our friendship, with our unintentional but inevitable competition on the job market being the work we did collaboratively that most tested and solidified our personal relationship.

Although we took only one graduate class together, we each had numerous opportunities for collaboration before we began collaborating ourselves. In Carrie's first graduate seminar, students produced an annotated bibliography interwoven with anecdotes about their own gendered writing experiences. All thirteen coauthors shared the excitement of seeing "Gender and Writing: Biblio(bio)graphical Stories" published that year. The following term, Carrie worked with a group of students and her professor to publish a collaborative interview with the author of a book they had read for the course. Similarly, much of Amy's graduate coursework encouraged collaboration. In one seminar, Amy collaborated with peers on a conference paper that analyzed the students' group dynamics in a graduate course. In a literacy seminar within the education department, the class compiled an edited collection of its projects juxtaposed with papers presented by visiting scholars. Amy also worked with the basic writing program to collaboratively author a sourcebook for the program's review.

There were also informal opportunities to collaborate. Our dissertation advisor held meetings with her advisees so that we could present our work in progress and comment on our peers' work. In addition, we both joined a small women's study group that had been meeting for several years. There we discussed readings on our exam lists, practiced for our orals, commented on prospectuses and conference proposals, and provided support during the dissertation and job-hunting phases of our careers. Collaborative work so thoroughly permeated our graduate training that we took it as the norm, at least in rhetoric and composition programs. When the journal *JAC* sought proposals for a special issue on collaboration and change in the academy, the editor was surprised by the number of people from our program who sent proposals. Perhaps this should have been our first inkling that our intensely collaborative graduate experience was not typical.

Not until we began preparing our materials for the job market did we see the possible costs of this collaboration. Responding to each other's job application letters in our dissertation group, we were shocked to find that our letters were strikingly similar, forcing us to realize that prospective employers would compare and choose among us. At that moment, Carrie felt a panicky need to distinguish herself and decided not to use university stationary for her letters.

The same thing happened with the red suits. On a collaborative shopping trip, Carrie talked Amy into buying a red suit and the next day bought one in a different style for herself. Then she promptly took it back, thinking it would be too easy for "them" to mix us up, even though we look nothing alike.[2] It was a premonition that ultimately came true, when we ended up having eight MLA interviews and three on-campus interviews with the same institutions. Indeed, a graduate student at the university where Carrie accepted a job later praised her presentation on student response to Toni Morrison—the presentation Amy gave. Another graduate student admitted that after we visited campus, he had voiced equal support for each of us—we seemed the same to him.

In retrospect, it is not surprising that we didn't become conscious of our need to compete until we began preparing our job applications. Until that point, there had been adequate resources to allow both of us to succeed. We both received grants to support our dissertation research. Both of our proposals for the *JAC* special issue on collaboration were accepted. We were both hired as research assistants for the rhetoric and composition program. Perhaps just as important, everyone who had previously completed a PhD in rhetoric and composition from our program had landed a tenure-track position. Although at that point we weren't conscious of a rationale for working together, we both assumed that our collaboration would make us more marketable.

It wasn't until we saw ourselves as prospective employers might that we had to confront some negative consequences of our collaboration. Worse than our worry that we would be seen as "the same" was the fear that they would look only at our differences and inevitably rank us. Our increasing awareness that others were choosing between us had the potential to affect the way we saw ourselves in relation to each other and in relation to the academy. As female graduate students who were the first in our families to go to college, we each fought tremors of self-doubt as we moved from an experience of academe as a wide-open prairie big enough for both of us to a sense that we were climbing a vertical ladder that narrowed as the rungs got higher.

Feminist scholars have recently begun to theorize the impact of competition between academic women. As Evelyn Fox Keller and Helene Moglen (1987) argue in their contribution to *Competition: A Feminist Taboo?,* academic women often have a more difficult time negotiating competition, particularly when they see competition and collaboration as binaries. Keller and Moglen suggest that this dualism prevents women from developing strategies to work through and with competition (34). In the same collection, Helen E. Longino (1987) articulates two very different models of competition. One is that of the race, where differences in ability lead to winners and losers—though everyone generally finishes and runners are often motivated to beat their best time, even if they aren't likely to win. The other image is that of the zero-sum game, exemplified by the game of baseball, where "the rules and structure of the competitive situation itself" means someone has to lose (249). As Longino sees it, the zero-sum game model of competition is based on an assumption of scarce resources and an ideology of individual ownership, and it is this version of competition that most feminists abhor as a "competitiveness forbidden by ideology." The challenge, then, is to harness the productive power of competition, to allow those with greater experience or skill to spur us to do our best work without losing our ability or desire to work with others rather than only in competition with them.

Though the tension between collaboration and competition is rarely discussed in the literature on graduate student professional development, it's a tension we experienced in graduate school as we worked to maintain a collaborative relationship while operating within an institutional structure forcing us to compete. In fact, choosing to collaborate—to work together, to help each other—was one way we sought to diffuse competitive feelings and to subvert the zero-sum game. As we have come to realize, a system based on the primacy of individual ambition will succeed only as individuals buy into the system. It takes a collaborative effort to change the system, especially when what we want to change are the constraints against collaboration. For us, collaboration meant—and continues to mean—a connection with each other as well as a struggle against the forces that threaten collaborative work.

When the *MLA Job List* was published in October, we identified our "dream jobs" and then agonized over the prospect that one of us would get the job that the other wanted. One way we dealt with these competitive feelings was by talking openly about our searches and by strategically sharing information. (Here *collusion* might seem a more appropriate term than *collaboration*.) For instance, when one of us would get a request for materials and the other wouldn't, we would help each other try to determine how our materials were being read. While our analysis may not have been accurate, pooling information gave us a sense of control over a process that, for the most part, was out of our control.

We again pooled information about the schools we would be interviewing with at MLA. We also decided to share a hotel room at the convention, against the recommendation of our peers, who thought that having to face each other at the end of a day of interviews might prove too stressful (although nothing proved as stressful as driving together in a blizzard to get to the conference in Toronto). One episode in particular illustrates the pain of trying to cooperate in an inevitably competitive venture. When Carrie returned to the hotel room after a day of interviews, she found that an invitation from the University of Nebraska for an on-campus interview had been left at the switchboard. Ecstatic at first, she then realized that she did not know whether the call had been for her or for Amy. When she checked, she found that the message had indeed been left for Amy. Carrie gave Amy the message and then left the room so as to avoid having to listen to Amy make plans for her interview, only to return to her hotel room to discover that although Nebraska had left the message in Amy's name, they were inviting both Amy and Carrie for campus interviews. The academic world was once again (this time somewhat literally) a wide-open prairie with room for us both. Until we remembered that only one of us could get the job.

The anxiety we felt over competing for the job at the University of Nebraska was connected to how we viewed ourselves as collaborative scholars. Part of the appeal of the Nebraska job stemmed from a recruitment letter sent to both of us before our MLA interview. This letter, signed by all three composition faculty, described their writing program in collaborative terms, emphasized the interconnected nature of teaching, scholarship, and service, and touted the opportunities for collaboration awaiting the person they would hire. As the job search went on, we realized how few jobs offered a potentially collaborative experience—even at places with established rhetoric and composition programs.

Somewhat ironically, our collaboration during the job search was seen by some search committees as a way of playing games with a process that was supposed to be secretive and individualistic (and in the control of the institution, not the job seeker). When we were the two candidates brought to campus for three schools, one school was left without a candidate for that year and ended up closing the search. Some recruitment committee members fumbled awkwardly at our references to our work together, seeming to want to ignore that we knew where the other was interviewing, perhaps so that the illusion of the individualistic competitive game could be maintained. But we not only knew where the other was interviewing, we debriefed each other about how our interviews had gone and gave each other tips on how to prepare for visits that we had already made. When Florida State called to tell Amy that they were offering the job to Carrie, the chair acknowledged, "Of course, you probably already know this." Carrie found out that Amy had received the Nebraska offer from a mutual friend who was baby-sitting while Carrie's husband picked her up at the airport. These moments were painful, but they would have been far more painful if we had not been committed to sharing information and maintaining our friendship. And it certainly helped that we both had early job offers. No doubt our commitment to collaboration would have been more sorely tried if only one of us had a successful job search. Indeed, Keller and Moglen tell a story of two women colleagues whose jobs at a state college involved heavy teaching loads that left them little time for their research. When one was offered a position at a more prestigious institution, her guilt over betraying her friend led her to decline (30).

Once we both signed job contracts, our collaboration entered a different stage. No longer competing against each other, we were competing madly against the clock to finish our dissertations, to move in opposite directions across the country, and to develop research programs. This is the point at which our dissertation writing became most overtly collaborative. What began as an occasional check-in phone call became a daily ritual. We'd report on what we had written, read aloud paragraphs, test out interpretations of data, and listen to alternate interpretations. We shared citations and almost shared a title, when our dissertation director suggested the same key words to both of us. The phone calls prompted us to return to our computers and solve whatever writing problems we were having. At this point, competition was a help rather than a hindrance—if one of us had been writing well, it spurred the other to get back to the keyboard. If we were in a race to finish, we were both going to cross that line.

It was during this time that Amy noticed a call for proposals for a collection of essays on feminism and composition. Looking forward to our soon-to-be futures as tenure-track faculty, we decided we wanted to have a new project in the works. And so began our first coauthored article. Our daily talking and writing together during the dissertation-writing phase made the prospect of coauthoring an article especially appealing. Not surprisingly, we decided to write about our recent experiences as part of a team that collaboratively revised the first-year writing curriculum and TA training program. Collaborating on this essay also enabled us to stay connected as friends and to support each other in our efforts toward gaining tenure. It provided a sense of community for us when we did not yet feel a part of the community we were working in. And feeling a part of a community was important—we'd been trained to think so.

Present

Which brings us to our "present tense": our current identities as faculty who continue to collaborate in all facets of our scholarly work. How did the sense of identity we developed through our collaborative professionalization in graduate school connect with, complicate, and contradict our expectations for our faculty lives? How is collaboration viewed by our current institutions? And what do our experiences mean for the ways that we mentor graduate students?

At the University of Nebraska, Lincoln (UNL), there is no official policy about collaboration and how it is evaluated for tenure and promotion. But true to the way the composition program at Nebraska advertised itself, opportunities for collaborative work abound. In Amy's first year, she and a colleague collaboratively designed a syllabus for a first-year writing course and met weekly as "teaching partners." The following semester, she and this colleague team-taught the introduction to composition theory and college teaching courses for new teaching assistants. During her first summer, Amy team-taught with three other faculty members in the Nebraska Writing Project. Collaboration is also the model for administration of the composition program—Amy and a colleague serve as co-coordinators of the first-year writing program, and they collaborate with two graduate student assistants in this work. Roughly half of Amy's publications are collaboratively authored, and she collaboratively writes with colleagues and graduate students.

While this world seems almost idyllic, Amy often faces the perception that collaboration is a practice wedded to the discipline of composition itself and is not the result of her individual choices as a teacher/scholar. In other words, because UNL composition faculty collaborate so heavily, there is a sense among some of Amy's colleagues that this is "something that those comp people do." This perception diminishes the extra energy that she and her colleagues expend not only in collaboration but also in providing evidence of its value in an institutional reward system that privileges individual status. Amy finds herself constantly trying to subvert institutional structures, such as the grant application that has only one line for a researcher or the Arts and Science form that has no way of valuing team-teaching. This identification of collaboration as an exclusively composition concern also has implications for graduate school programs, where one group of students is likely to be encouraged to collaborate while other students are not. Despite Amy's ongoing collaborative work in every area of intellectual inquiry, collaboration still is not viewed by department colleagues as especially valuable for graduate student professionalization.

Like Amy, Carrie sought opportunities for collaboration when she arrived at Florida State. As director of the reading/writing center, she worked closely with the director of the first-year writing program to train and supervise the 100 graduate teaching assistants who taught in their program, and she regularly collaborated with her graduate assistants to create teachers' guides, run staff meetings, plan research, and prepare conference presentations. But though Carrie was praised in her annual evaluations for her ability to work cooperatively, she was also warned to limit her collaboration with colleagues on scholarly work. She knew from discussions with other department members that such collaboration was viewed as nepotism, especially when junior faculty collaborated with senior colleagues (calling into question whether the term *colleague* should really apply when a hierarchical relationship is assumed).

Although the official promotion and tenure guidelines at Florida State allow for collaboration, they also make clear that collaboration is acceptable only in some areas of English studies and that the person who collaborates must make special efforts to "seek advice early and often about how the department is perceiving your independent reputation." The guidelines offer this more specific warning:

> While the Department recognizes the value of collaborative projects, we emphasize the importance of establishing an independent reputation. The Department has no guidelines about what proportion of your work should be independently authored, but you are undoubtedly in a better position if you have some clearly definable texts of your own in print (articles and book chapters) when you are considered for tenure.

As Carrie prepared to go up for tenure, she was asked several times by colleagues who supported her case how many of her published articles were singly authored. Given that a colleague whose scholarship was heavily collaborative had been recently denied tenure, they had a right to be wary. An additional cause for concern was the provost's public declaration that he would make sure that high tenure standards were applied, and for most faculty in the humanities, high standards means one thing: a singly-authored book (or books) from a well-regarded university press.

So why do we collaborate? Because, to borrow an old expression, you can take the girls out of the collaborative community, but you can't take the collaborative community out of the girls. Those early opportunities shaped our sense of who we are as professionals, as teachers, researchers, administrators, and mentors. Although we have produced and will continue to produce individually authored work, the stimulation we get out of working together—and with others—helps us feel at home in a profession that functions more often like a narrow ladder than like a wide-open plain. Our continuing collaboration also helps us to get things done. Because we want to help advance each other's career as much as our own, we are motivated by our accountability to each other. And the work can go forward even when our administrative loads or teaching loads or family responsibilities demand our immediate attention. One week Carrie does more work on our research project, and the next week Amy does more work. Such an arrangement has been especially important because each of us has had a baby since we've taken our jobs and neither had her tenure clock delayed.

Future

We started this essay by promising to explain how and why we collaborated throughout our graduate training and into our professional careers. But a larger question remains: Should we foster collaborative practices within the graduate programs we're now part of? Given the competitive job market, the hierarchical structure of most departments and universities, and the scarce-resources model of rewards in higher education, do we dare tout the benefits of collaboration? Well, yes, of course. The difference, though, is that we need to articulate clear rationales for scholarly collaboration and, at the same time, let students know that collaboration is still a risky enterprise—one that might mean working harder and publishing more and being asked to spend a chunk of your precious research time crafting rhetorically savvy justifications for your collaborative work. In spite of these challenges, we believe there are clear philosophical, personal, and political reasons to advocate collaboration throughout graduate training.

First, there is the philosophical argument that language, knowledge-making, and text production are inevitably social and collaborative processes so we might as well make the process explicit rather than hidden. Patricia Sullivan (1994) points to the dissertation in particular as a site of this inevitable collaboration: "The institutional contexts that frame and circumscribe the processes of the writer locate the dissertation in a social context that is fundamentally collaborative. The author of the text literally writes the text *with* others" (25). But since this argument doesn't provide sufficient justification for collaborative work to those outside social constructionist circles, especially when done by those who have not yet proven themselves as "independent" scholars, we also want to point out that there are personal benefits to collaborative work. For example, Janine Rider and Esther Broughton (1994) describe how they began their collaboration when they both worked as adjuncts alienated from the rest of the department, their collaboration continuing when they decided to pursue PhDs at a distant university, even though it meant being separated from their families for months at a time. For these women, collaboration gave them the support they needed to forge professional identities and take up academic challenges.

Collaborative work has provided the same kind of support for us and for many who were our peers in graduate school and who have now gone on to academic careers. In one meeting of our graduate student study group, when the subject of quitting graduate school came up, we were surprised to discover that each of us had quit school once, for a myriad of reasons that could be boiled down to the fact that we didn't feel we belonged. Collaboration gave us a way to feel we were making over the academy in our own image—making the place more like a place where we *wanted* to belong.

Rider and Broughton's (1994) collaboration also served as a means of interrogating existing institutional structures when they went so far as to propose coauthoring a dissertation (249). Although their proposal was not successful, it brought to the attention of faculty and students the institutional structures that inhibit collaborative work, a necessary first step in the process of changing those structures. Indeed, Ervin and Fox (1994) see collaboration as a means of political action, a means of taking "responsibility for the structures of our own institutions, structures that determine our professional identities and activities" (54). It is these same structures that we continue to struggle to transform.

So we say again, yes, we should encourage graduate students to collaborate, but we hope also to make students aware that the kind of collaboration we advocate is that which is intentional, theorized, potentially subversive—not "natural," not "inevitable," and not without consequences.

Postscript

In the spring of 2000, Amy Goodburn was recommended for tenure and promotion to associate professor of English at the University of Nebraska, Lincoln, where she continues to collaborate on a wide range of projects. In spite of receiving the strong support of her department, Carrie Leverenz was ultimately denied tenure at Florida State University. Because current university policy forbids promotion and tenure committees from meeting to discuss cases (committee members cast ballots privately), there is no way to know how collaborative research was evaluated. Carrie continues to collaborate, however, with Amy and with others, in her new position as associate professor and director of composition at Texas Christian University.

End Notes

1. According to an MLA census of job placement rates for PhDs completed in 1996–1997, only 33.6 percent found tenure-track employment (Laurence 1998). For rhetoric and composition specialists, that number was somewhat better—64 percent.

2. If it seems a stretch to think that job candidates are distinguished by their clothing, one of Carrie's colleagues who was in her MLA interview remembered telling the others on the interview team that she liked the one in the red coat.

Chapter Fourteen

In Search of My "Jingle"

Reconciling Voice and Identity After the Dissertation Defense

Sheila L. Carter-Tod

Many of the chapters in this volume deal with decisions made while writing the dissertation. The writers articulate and wrestle with issues of identity and voice that arise when writing a document that not only allows entrance into a scholarly arena but also announces the writer's emergence as scholar. Janis Haswell sees dissertation mentoring as helpful to her construction of voice. Fred Arroyo describes being able to make a place within the field for his position, being able to secure membership as a scholar. Cindy Moore and Peggy Woods likewise come to some resolution. Woods clearly articulates this resolution when she says to Moore:

> It seems that as dissertation writers, we are involved in this process of re-visioning—not only re-visioning who we are, but re-visioning our own voices. . . . I wonder if we could take things even a bit further and say the dissertation itself is not only an act of re-vision, but a process of reconciliation. As we work to re-vision our selves and our voices, it seems we are also simultaneously engaged in the process of reconciling all the identities we have and had as well as all the voices we speak with. (74)

In these cases, dissertation writers resolve difficult issues, reconcile conflicting identities. But what happens when we do not reach resolution and reconciliation? What happens when a dissertator begins to articulate struggle but out of lack of courage or time does not resolve it? When we (as doctoral candidates) do not acknowledge, explore, and address the issues of academic voice and identity within our dissertations, we can create a postdissertation situation in which these unresolved issues hinder our ability to reconnect with the making of knowledge within the academic community. Without a sense of self or voice, we can at best discuss and refute theories proposed by others, but not actually create or shape our discipline. In this chapter, I want to examine this problem through my own resolution of the questions of identity and voice, a resolution that came after, not during, the writing of my dissertation.

One of my daughter's favorite storybooks is called *The Jester Has Lost His Jingle*. I love reading this story to her, and when it came time to think about this chapter, the story, about a jester banished from court because he is no longer able to make the king laugh, kept coming back to me. Feeling as though he has lost what he sees as his purpose in life (the ability to make others laugh), the jester goes off on a journey to find a sense of humor and to bring back laughter to the kingdom. The journey takes the jester "far and wide" and "near and far" until he finally discovers the true source of laughter and runs back to the kingdom to pass his newfound discovery on to the king and the other subjects of the court.

I've struggled with the implications of choosing a jester to represent my journey, and my identification with this tale isn't so much with the jester himself as with this idea of a journey, a search for voice and identity. My own journey didn't start with banishment but with the writing of and subsequent successful defense of a dissertation. Yet this was a beginning, a success, that I, like many graduate students, experienced as a challenge to, and maybe even loss of, identity and voice. John M. Ackerman, in "Postscript: The Assimilation and Tactics of Nate" (1995), articulates some of these challenges when he writes, "What is graduate school for many students but a struggle for identity in a contested professional space defined by genre activity, quarrels over epistemology and method, and a search for affiliation?" (145). The successful completion and defense of a dissertation doesn't always neatly conclude and resolve this struggle but instead intensifies it.

The Dissertation

When he started his routine,
And strutted on the stage,
How could he have known
That the king was in a rage?
—David Saltzman (1995), *The Jester Has Lost His Jingle*

My dissertation looked at the writing practices of English as a second language (ESL) students and the role that the writing center played in those writing practices. The format was traditional. I conducted interviews with participants and tutors throughout the semester of data collection, observed tutoring sessions, and collected and analyzed texts produced by the student participants. I now identify this process of research and analysis as the beginning of my journey. My work with ESL students, plus my subsequent analysis of their texts and their experiences in creating and revising those texts, forced me to voice specific conflicts related to voice and identity. These were conflicts I not only discussed in my dissertation but experienced in the writing of it. However, many of the decisions that I made in order to complete my dissertation led me further from instead of closer to a resolution.

For example, early in my proposal defense, I was searching for a framework for focusing some of my data collection. I had actually found such a framework within a story that my mother had told me. Storytelling to convey insight and understanding is deeply rooted in both my culture as an African American and in my family. My committee, however, as an extension of the academy that requires sources and methodologies recognized by the academy, found the story "problematic," sending me back to my research data in an attempt to find a similar idea from a "credible" source. I was able to mention my mother's story but had to merge it with outside sources, thereby hybridizing both my voice as a writer and my way of knowing.

Some may say that such a hybrid voice—created when ideas and forms of expression outside those deemed appropriate by the American academic community are grafted onto the expectations of academic writing—is a natural part of the evolutionary process of becoming a scholar. Some say that the ability to linguistically move in and out of the language of our field is a mark of academic competence or that the hybridization we practice during the dissertation process does not have to dictate our future scholarship. This may indeed be true for some, but it wasn't for me. After being awarded a PhD, even while enjoying being professionally active and seeking to investigate traditional issues in very nontraditional ways, I continued to experience what Alexis De Veaux described experiencing as she completed her doctorate: an "ever present feeling of being an outsider within the halls of academe . . .[with] tears of frustration and bouts of self-doubt . . . [and] the anger as a writer trying to prove that I can indeed write in 'scholarly' language even if it is at the price of my own voice" (1995, 68).

My dissertation experience with hybridization also seemed to parallel the experiences of the ESL students I was studying. For instance, there was Junko,[1] a senior Japanese student, whose teacher told her that the organization of her senior project should emerge from the topic Junko chose, yet when Junko organized her project in the form she felt best explored her topic of Japanese theater, the teacher told her the piece lacked clear organization. "I guess she meant that I could organize my paper any American way that I wanted to," Junko said. I understood her struggle, but I also understood her desire to do well in her English course. I explained that her organizational structure was not "wrong" in and of itself, but that it did not fit into what was expected of her at this American college. She replied, "They accepted me knowing that I was Japanese. If they wanted someone to use Japanese topics and American forms, then an American student could have used an encyclopedia. It is difficult to think Japanese and make it fit into English language and American forms."

What could I say to her when my experiences with standard academic English had been so similar? Had I not seen the forms of expression that had been shaped by my family stories, and my readings of storytellers, be put in their "nonstandard" place? Had I not watched my own work be edited by others "for better form," feeling the life revised out of my own writing "for coherence"? Did I not watch, with frustration and helplessness, as my committee imposed what seemed like *its* form and organizational patterns on *my* study? I wanted to say that I shared her feelings. I wanted to say that perhaps she should go and make her teacher understand her feelings so that the teacher might broaden her concept of this particular rhetorical form. Instead I said, "I do understand" and went on to explain what was expected. My actions did nothing to create a space for her unique voice, but instead colluded with the oppressive force under which we both struggled. Our time together was then spent with me teaching her the technique of voice hybridization.

In a CCCC round table on the dissertation, held shortly after my dissertation defense and this meeting with Junko, I voiced the questions I was still unable to answer: Could I have, in some way small or large, pushed harder to open avenues that may allow for other forms, other voices, in the dissertation or even in the classroom? Did I simply assume for the sake of time and the need to complete the degree that there was no way of changing the dissertation? What exactly had I lost and what had I gained? Looking back on these questions, I realize I did view completing the degree as worth the price of voice and, subsequently, identity. I gave up more than the ability to credit my mother with her story. With each revision that standardized my voice and speech pattern, I surrendered more confidence in the language and forms that had shaped my world and ideas. I accepted that my language and structure were nonstandard and, therefore, unacceptable for entrance into the realm of "scholarly academic writing." I revised myself out of the piece. Like the dissertator in Marilyn Urion's chapter who says, "I [thought] I could make the work be what I wanted it to after I got through the program" (7), I convinced myself that once I was a fully credentialed scholar, I would have more opportunity to enact change; therefore, the battle was better left until after the degree was completed.

What I did not realize was that in putting off resolution of these issues of voice and identity, I was turning my back on what had been the source material for my sense of voice and identity—my family and my culture. Doing so, I began to lose sight of the reasons I had chosen composition as my field of study and what I had seen as possible within it.

Leaving the Field

My passion has always been language and empowerment. I am acutely aware of ways in which people write themselves into being and in doing so give voice to their own experience and the experiences of others. When I began teaching composition during my master's degree program, the theory and practice of composition transformed me. As a graduate student, I was also, as Alys Culhane describes in her chapter, shaped by expressivists such as Peter Elbow and Ken Macrorie and "social constructionists" such as James Berlin and Kenneth Bruffee. I had tried on various voices and worked with various interpretive models through explorations in literary theory. I'd begun to reconcile the idea that voice was something discovered within, with the idea that meaning and voice are shaped or even discerned in our interactions with others. In the classroom and in my graduate seminars, I'd enjoyed working with students as they recognized and found confidence in their own voices while working with them to help them revise in a way that developed the expression of voice. I had always loved teaching writing.

However, upon completing a dissertation that was not an experience in developing voice and confidence, I fell back on traditional ways of teaching academic writing; I spent more and more time teaching conventions instead of opening opportunities to explore the questions. Frustrated and still not fully clear about who I was in the broader academic environment, I decided to leave the composition classroom entirely. I accepted an administrative faculty position. I felt some security in the idea of a position that was in an academic community but required a very different type of writing. I believed that within this writing realm, I would not have to deal with reestablishing my own voice because the grants and reports had prescribed formats and a set audience.

And so, after working for four years as ESL academic coordinator and an assistant professor of English at a small, private, liberal arts, women's college, I took a position as coordinator of reading and assessment at a large land-grant university. The position provided me with a great deal of work in a challenging and rewarding environment, just the distraction I thought I needed. I was perfectly comfortable writing grants, developing retention programs, and working with students and faculty to implement those programs. That is, until one day when a young African American student named Barishah came to my office.

Reconnection

Barishah was a senior English major who originally came to me for assistance with reading. After some testing and conferencing we both realized that, as was the case with most students with whom I worked, she had no difficulties with speed or comprehension. We then focused our attention on time management skills. We looked over her week's reading and writing assignments, and we set up a study schedule. But Barishah, an extremely bright student, was struggling with more than issues of time management. Near the end of one of our sessions (just as I was about to recommend that she work with her advisor or with the writing center, which could provide more focused assistance than my office was designed to give), Barishah asked me about an essay she had been reading on the use of Black English. She had been given an assignment to write about her personal position on the material being discussed. She looked at me and said, "I wanted to talk to you because you act like you want me to understand and because you used to teach this stuff, didn't you?"

That one question kicked off a long discussion that tossed me back into the issues I'd taken this job to avoid. Barishah explained to me her challenges as one of very few African Americans in the English department, the feeling that what she wanted to say could not be understood. Barishah was not so different from Junko or from me. What lesson was I going to provide for her to take away? From what voice would I speak? Would I fall back on a lifeless hybrid voice that I had found so defeating? Could we work with what I had learned to make a broadened perspective? And what else had taken place within the field of composition since I'd completed my dissertation? What alternative modes of expressions had other dissertation writers opened up?[2] This small encounter was pivotal in starting me once again on a journey to seek voice, identity, and reconnection.

Until this point, I viewed my acceptance as a scholar in composition and rhetoric much in the same way that the jester views his relationship to the king—as if there was some monarch out there dictating the acceptability of expression and banishing those who did not entertain his notion of what voice was correct. I absorbed the guidance and correction offered by my dissertation committee (all people I accepted as representative of academe) as if they spoke as king. This didn't begin with the dissertation. On reflection, I see I spent most of my academic career working to make sure I adhered to some kingly authority of acceptable academic discourse. It wasn't surprising, then, that the dissertation should bring about my final acquiescence to some authority of acceptable academic discourse. Yet, having acquiesced—and even taught students to edit out self—I was no more a part of the throne than before.

My experience with Barishah forced me to stop and consider (this time from a different perspective) the possibility of honoring other community practices and norms as acceptable academic discourse. Who defines, shapes, and redefines the field so that it is more open to students like Barishah? Hadn't I passed all of the requirements that should have formally made me an active member and contributor to the field? I had to assert my right and ability to question the king—that is, the norms of acceptable academic discourse—if I could even begin to envision myself as shaping and not simply being shaped by my chosen field.

In the children's story, the pivotal point for the jester occurs when he meets a young girl who is dying and who asks him what there is to laugh about in her world. Fumbling for an answer he cannot find out there, the jester finally realizes that his ability to guide her toward laughter is found within him and her. It is at that point that he is able to help make her laugh, and in making her laugh, he sees that he has not lost his jingle. Instead he needed to trust his ability to make people find joy from within. Armed with this insight he heads back to the kingdom. While my realization does not completely parallel that of the jester, Barishah did provide a key turning point for my journey, urging me to actively define my role in the process of shaping and creating a space for voice. Barishah brought me, like the jester, to the point of looking within because I had not found the answers outside myself.

I did agree to work with Barishah. However, this time I did not shy away from the issues being raised nor did I simply teach her to use the conventions provided. Instead we met regularly and looked at what she was reading and what she wanted to say in her essays. I helped her to retain her voice while still meeting the teacher's requirements. We also talked about some of my difficulties with the same issues, and in our time together I helped her to see that there were areas for negotiation that legitimized other forms of expression.

With that experience, my desire to make this change possible for others was rekindled. I decided to return to the classroom, this time not to teach established conventions with the goal of producing students proficient in the practices of academic English, but to empower students to write themselves into being, to give voice to their own experiences and the experiences of others. In other words, I was beginning to reconcile some of the identities I had only let emerge previously as either/or.

A Return to the Teaching of Composition

When an associate professor's position at a local community college came available, I took it. Numerous layoffs had taken place in area plants, and as a result, workers were allowed (as part of the Federal Trade Act) to return to school. The idea of working with students (mostly women) who had been working in factories for years (some as many as twenty-five years) seemed challenging and exciting. These women were new to higher education, new to writing, and new to the concept that what they had to say mattered. They were aware that there were accepted conventions of academic English, but they viewed the entire writing process as yet another defeating situation. I tried to demystify the conventions of standard English. I encouraged them across genres to value what they had to say and—even in the midst of revision and corrections—to hold on to how they wanted their thoughts expressed.

I remember one particular student who sought feedback on a story she wrote outside of class. Her story, about a family reunion in a southwestern Virginia hollow, was a powerful weaving of humor and tragedy that intricately intertwined her family's speech patterns with the events of the story. She quietly waited for everyone to leave class before she asked me to read the story and then quickly left. When I got back to my office and began reading the story I realized I would need to talk to her to get a real feel for what she wanted to capture. I asked her to come by my office and through the time that we spent together discussing the family reunion and the specifics of the individuals in the story, I was able to give her productive responses on how to revise her piece and retain her voice. Though she was not writing for a grade, I mentored her the way I wished my dissertation advisors had done.

In classroom encounters such as this, my community college teaching provided me with many opportunities to discuss openly the connection among voice, identity, and writing. In these classes, we explored the power issues inherent in peer workshops and the ways in which certain "weaker" writers wholly accept the feedback of someone they feel "says things better" or "is a better writer." Working with students both in and out of the classroom helped me to continue to reconcile my own sense of the importance of certain academic writing conventions with the importance of finding, retaining, and developing voice. But while immersion in this teaching helped me define my role in the academy, it left the issue of my own voice in the larger community of composition unresolved. In this community college, teaching was the focus, and with five classes a semester, it almost had to be. I was not actively participating in the research community and I missed it. You see, it was not enough for the jester to find the joy within, he then needed to go back to the kingdom and convince the king that he had not lost his jingle. I needed to take my voice to a place in the larger academic community.

A Full Return

"We've found where it's been hiding.
We've discovered where it's been.
It's hiding inside everyone!
It's buried deep within!

Laughter's like a seedling,
Waiting patiently to sprout.
All it takes is just a push
To make it pop right out."

—David Saltzman (1995), *The Jester Has Lost His Jingle*

My latest career decision has been to return to teaching in a large land-grant university. My current post provides me with opportunities to investigate issues of voice and identity in the field of composition, and in my current position, I not only can encourage and empower writers like Barishah and Junko, I also can challenge some of the conventions that honor and justify reproducing the status quo. All tension between academic and personal/cultural voices has not gone away, but I am no longer looking for or to someone else to clarify my position on this issue. If my dissertation writing and defense challenged my very sense of identity and voice, my journey since has been about the various career decisions that I've made in an attempt to regain that identity and fit my goals for scholarship into a larger academic perspective. My academic self, voice, and identity are issues that must be reconciled from within as I work with teachers and students like Junko and Barishah and the woman from southwestern Virginia who share my questions and struggles. The career choices that I make must be dictated by my desire to shape the academic community in such a way as to make it a place where I and all of my students can comfortably participate.

The roles have reversed for me now, and I am advising doctoral students who are researching and writing their own dissertations. In this capacity, I energetically embrace wrestling with and questioning voice and identity, the conflicts inherent in the writing of a dissertation. In meetings with doctoral students, I try to give voice to the too often unspoken struggle between the need to clarify and the need to retain self and voice within the broader scope of the discipline. I also encourage the conversation toward resolution. While I do not attempt to provide my advisees with the answers, I do communicate my journey and remind them that "where laughter's [or voice or identity's] hiding . . . It's hiding inside of YOU!" (Saltzman). It's part of my role to offer this reminder, and doing so, I create a broader academic community—one in which I and others can participate, challenge, and, when necessary, redefine. My career choices took me on a journey that brought me back to a sense of who I am and what my role is in the larger academic setting. This chapter gives voice to that process and in doing so recaptures my own voice.

I can't say that my struggles have been fully resolved, and like me, other contributors to this book are still trying to resolve the questions of voice and identity. Our common experience with the difficulty of openly raising and discussing these questions while writing the dissertation leads me to believe that, unlike the story of the jester, the larger community of composition and rhetoric has not openly proclaimed, "You've saved the day! You've brought back love and laughter and helped us find the way!" There is still reluctance about broadening the perimeters of established practice. There is still reluctance to listen to the voices of students.

Examining the experiences of students of color in a first-year writing class at the University of Minnesota, Carol A. Miller (1997) found students often felt that academic success meant sacrificing both culture and expression. In response, Miller argues:

> We must perform an ongoing reexamination of our pedagogical objectives and instructional strategies, especially their consequences for students who may logically resist being socially reconstructed when that process involves behaviors of assimilation and acculturation. (297)

I echo this call for pedagogical reexamination and suggest that it extend beyond the composition classroom to the larger field of composition and rhetoric, including the dissertation. The dissertation process is a rich, provocative scholarly endeavor that announces one's introduction into the academic field—and by reenvisioning voice and identity in the dissertation, we redefine the scope of the field so that students like myself can enter as whole participants.

End Notes

1. All student names have been changed.

2. Many of this collection's authors explore how they too worked within the constraints of the traditional dissertation while others, such as Darrell Fike and Peggy Woods, experienced more freedom of form and expression. These dissertators challenged the very structure establishing what is and is not accepted as authoritative scholarly form. Knowing that others have already made these challenges gave me some comfort and security as I voiced in this chapter what I had struggled with but not resolved in my own dissertation.

Works Cited

Ackerman, J. 1995. "Postscript: The Assimilation and Tactics of Nate." In *Genre Knowledge in Disciplinary Communication: Cognition, Culture, Power*, eds. C. Berkenkotter and T. Huckin, 145–50. Hillsdale, NJ: Lawrence Erlbaum.

Aisenberg, N., and M. Harrington. 1988. *Women of Academe: Outsiders in the Sacred Grove*. Amherst: University of Massachusetts Press.

Anderson, J. 1993. *Deaf Students Mis-Writing, Teacher Mis-Reading: English Education and the Deaf College Student*. Burtonville, MD: Linstock.

Anson, C. M., and C. Rutz. 1998. "Graduate Students, Writing Programs, and Consensus-Based Management: Collaboration in the Face of Disciplinary Ideology." *WPA: Writing Program Administration* 21: 106 –20.

Atkins, G. D. 1992. *Estranging the Familiar: Toward a Revitalized Critical Writing*. Athens: University of Georgia Press.

Bakhtin, M. M. 1981. *The Dialogic Imagination*, trans. C. Emerson and M. Holquist, ed. M. Holquist. Austin: University of Texas Press.

Baird, L. 1990. "The Melancholy of Anatomy: The Personal and Professional Development of Graduate and Professional School Students." In *Higher Education: Handbook of Theory and Research*, 6: 361–92. New York: Agathon Press.

Barth, J. [1968] 1995. "Lost in the Funhouse." In *The Story and Its Writer: An Introduction to Short Fiction*, ed. A. Carters, 105–22. Boston: Bedford Books.

Bartholomae, D. 1985. "Inventing the University." In *When a Writer Can't Write: Studies in Writer's Block and Other Composing Process Problems*, ed. M. Rose, 135–65. New York: Guilford.

———. 1996. "What Is Composition and (if you know what that is) Why Do We Teach It?" In *Composition in the Twenty-First Century: Crisis and*

Change, eds. L. Z. Bloom, D. A. Dailer, and E. M. White, 11–28. Carbondale, IL: Southern Illinois University Press.

Beecher, C. 1977. *A Treatise on Domestic Economy.* New York: Schoken Books.

Benjamin, J. 1988. *The Bonds of Love: Psychoanalysis, Feminism, and the Problem of Domination.* New York: Pantheon.

Berkenkotter, C., T. N. Huckin, and J. Ackerman. 1988. "Conventions, Conversations, and the Writer: Case Study of a Student in a Rhetoric Ph.D. Program." *Research in the Teaching of English* 22 (1): 9–41.

Bérubé, M. 1996. "Against Subjectivity." *PMLA* 111: 1063–68.

Bishop, W. 1997. "Alternate Styles for Who, What, Why?" In *Elements of Alternate Style,* ed. W. Bishop, 3–10. Portsmouth, NH: Boynton/Cook.

Boese, C. 1998–2000. "The Ballad of the Internet Nutball: Chaining Rhetorical Visions from the Margins of the Margins to the Mainstream of the Xenaverse." Diss. Rensselaer Polytechnic Institute. http://www.nutball.com/dissertation (21 June 2002).

Bouletreau, V. 2001. Personal email. 12 March.

Bourdieu, P. 1991. *Language and Symbolic Power,* trans. G. Raymond and M. Adamson. Cambridge, MA: Harvard University Press.

Bowen, W. G., and N. L. Rudenstine. 1992. In *Pursuit of the Ph.D.* Princeton: Princeton University Press.

Bridwell-Bowles, L. 1992. "Discourse and Diversity: Experimental Writing Within the Academy." *College Composition and Communication* 43: 349–67.

Brodkey, L. 1989. "On the Subject of Class and Gender." *College English* 55: 125–41.

Brueggemann, B. J. 1996. "Still-Life: Representations and Silences in the Participant-Observer Role." In *Ethics and Representation in Qualitative Studies of Literacy*, eds. P. Mortensen and G. E. Kirsch, 17–39. Urbana, IL: National Council of Teachers of English.

Bruns, G. 1991. "What is Tradition?" *New Literary History* 22: 1–21.

Burke, K. 1950. *A Rhetoric of Motives*. New York: Prentice-Hall.

Caplan, P. J. 1995. *Lifting a Ton of Feathers: A Woman's Guide to Surviving in the Academic World*. Toronto: University of Toronto Press.

Cargnelutti, T. 2001. Personal email. 12 March.

Carlton, S. B. 1994. "Voice and the Naming of Woman." In *Voices on Voice*, ed. K. B. Yancey, 226–41. Urbana, IL: National Council of Teachers of English.

Carr, C. 1997. *Angel of Darkness*. New York: Random House.

Cliff, M. 1988. "A Journey into Speech." In *The Graywolf Annual Five: Multi-Cultural Literacy,* eds. R. Simonson and S. Walker, 57–62. St. Paul: Graywolf Press.

Code, L. 1995. *Rhetorical Spaces: Essays on Gendered Locations*. New York: Routledge.

Collins, P. H. 1991. *Black Feminist Thought: Knowledge, Consciousness, and the Politics of Empowerment*. New York: Routledge.

Cook, S. 1997. "Tips to Help Women on Campus Get Published." *Women in Higher Education* 6 (9): 23.

Connors, R., and A. Lunsford. 1988. "Frequency of Formal Errors in Current College Writing, or Ma & Pa Kettle Do Research." *College Composition and Communication* 39: 395–409.

Cooper, M. 1994. "Dialogic Learning Across Disciplines." *Journal of Advanced Composition* 14: 531–46.

———. 1997. "Postmodern Ethics in the Writing Classroom." Paper presented at the Conference on College Composition and Communication, Phoenix, March 13–15.

———. 1999. "Postmodern Pedagogy in Electronic Conversations." In *Passions, Pedagogies, and 21st Century Technologies*, eds. G. E. Hawisher and C. L. Selfe, 140–60. Urbana, IL: National Council of Teachers of English.

Damrosch, D. 2000. "Mentors and Tormentors in Doctoral Education." *Chronicle of Higher Education Online* 17 Nov. http://chronicle.com (21 June 2002).

De Veaux, A. 1995. "The Third Degree: Black Women Scholars Storming the Ivory Tower." *Essence* 25 (12): 68.

Denzin, N. K., and Y. S. Lincoln. 1994. *Handbook of Qualitative Research.* Thousand Oaks, CA: Sage.

Derrida, J. 1978. "Structure, Sign, and Play in the Discourse of the Human Sciences." In *Writing and Difference*, trans. A. Bass. Chicago: University of Chicago Press.

Dissertation Consortium. 2001. "Challenging Tradition: A Conversation about the Dissertation in Rhetoric and Composition." *College Composition and Communication* 52: 441–54.

Dixon, K. 1995. "Gendering the Personal." *College Composition and Communication* 46: 255–75.

Dobratz, S. 2001. Personal email. 12 March.

Dorwick, K. 1996–1998. "Building the Virtual Department: A Case Study of Online Teaching and Research." Diss. University of Illinois at Chicago. http://www.uic.edu/depts/engl/projects/dissertations/kdorwick/toc.htm (21 June 2002).

DuPlessis, R. B. 1990. *The Pink Guitar: Writing as Feminist Practice.* New York: Routledge.

Ede, L., and A. A. Lunsford. 2001. "Collaboration and Concepts of Authorship." *PMLA* 16: 354–69.

Elbow, P. 1987. "Closing My Eyes as I Speak: An Argument for Ignoring Audience." *College English* 49: 50–69.

———. 1991. "Reflections on Academic Discourse: How It Relates to Freshmen and Colleagues." *College English* 53: 135–55.

———. 1990. *What Is English?* New York and Urbana, IL: Modern Language Associaton and National Council of Teachers of English.

Enos, T. 1996. *Gender Roles and Faculty Lives in Rhetoric and Composition.* Carbondale: Southern Illinois University Press.

Ervin, E., and D. L. Fox. 1994. “Collaboration as Political Action.” *JAC* 14: 53–71.

ETD 2001: Fourth International Symposium on Electronic Theses and Dissertations. California Institute of Technology, Pasadena, CA.: 22–24 March 2001. http://library.caltech.edu/etd/ (21 June 2002).

Fort, K. 1971. “Form, Authority, and the Critical Essay.” *College English* 32: 629–39.

Foucault, M. 1972. *The Archeology of Knowledge*, trans. A. M. Sheridan Smith. New York: Pantheon.

———. 1983. “The Subject and Power.” In *Michel Foucault: Beyond Structuralism and Hermeneutics*, eds. H. L. Dreyfus and P. Rabinow, 208–26. Chicago: University of Chicago Press.

Fox, E., G. McMillan, and J. Eaton. 1999. *The Evolving Genre of Electronic Theses and Dissertations*. http://www.ndltd.org/pubs/Genre.htm#UMIa (21 June 2002).

Freire, P. 1996. *Letters to Cristina*. New York: Routledge.

Freisinger, R. R. 1994. “Voicing the Self: Toward a Pedagogy of Resistance in a Postmodern Age.” In *Voices on Voice: Perspectives, Definitions, Inquiry*, ed. K. B. Yancey, 242–75. Urbana, IL: National Council of Teachers of English.

Freud, S. 1949. *An Outline of Psycho-Analysis*, Standard ed., trans. and ed. J. Strachey. New York: Norton.

Fulwiler, T. 1994. “Looking and Listening for My Voice.” In *Landmark Essays on Voice and Writing*, eds. P. Elbow, 157–64. Mahwah, NJ: Hermagorus Press.

Gadamer, H. G. 1984. “The Hermeneutics of Suspicion.” In *Hermeneutics: Questions and Prospects*, eds. G. Shapiro and A. Sica, 54–65. Amherst: University of Massachusetts Press.

Gennep, A. van. [1908] 1960. “Initiation Rites.” In *The Rites of Passage*, trans. M. B. Vizedom and G. L. Caffee. Chicago: University of Chicago Press, Phoenix Books.

Giddings, P. 1984. *When and Where I Enter: The Impact of Black Women on Race and Sex in America*. New York: William Morrow.

Gradin, S. L. 2000. "Revitalizing Romantics, Pragmatics, and Possibilities for Teaching. *College English* 62: 403–7.

———. 1994. *Romancing Rhetorics: Social Perspectives on the Teaching of Writing*. Portsmouth, NH: Boynton/Cook.

Graduate Research Network 2002. 2001. Call for Proposals. http://www2.gasou.edu/facstaff/jwalker/cfp/cw2002/2002.html (21 June 2002).

Griffin, G. 1995. *Season of the Witch*. Pasadena, CA: Trilogy Books.

Grigar, D., and J. Barber. 1997. "Defending Your Life in MOOspace: A Report from the Electronic Edge." *High Wired: Negotiating the Tight/Trope of Educational MOOs*, ed. C. Haynes and J. R. Holmevik, 192–231. Ann Arbor: University of Michigan Press.

Gubar, S. 1999. "The Graying of Professor Bombeck." *College English* 61: 431–47.

H.D. 1961. *Helen of Egypt*. New York: New Directions.

Hamilton, R. G. 1993. "On the Way to the Professoriate: The Dissertation." *New Directions in Teaching and Learning* 54 (Summer): 47–56.

Hanson, M. 1986. "Development Concepts of Voice in Case Studies of College Students: The Owned Voice and Authoring (Writing)." Diss. Harvard University.

Haswell, R. H. 1991. *Gaining Ground in College Writing: Tales of Development and Interpretation*. Dallas: Southern Methodist University Press.

Hays, J. 1987. "The Development of Discursive Maturity in College Writers." In *A Sourcebook for Basic Writing Teachers*, ed. T. Enos, 480–96. New York: Random House.

Holbrooke, S. E. 1991. "Women's Work: The Feminizing of Composition Studies." *Rhetoric Review* 9: 201–29.

hooks, b. 1989. *Talking Back: Thinking Feminist, Thinking Black*. Boston: South End Press.

Howie, G., and A. Tauchert. 1999. "Oddfellows: The Female Subject of Academia." Paper presented at the Gender and Education Conference at the University of Warwick, UK, March 1999. Summarized and quoted in S. Cook, "Female Academics Perpetuate Traditional Male 'Standards.'" *Women in Higher Education*, 8 (5): 1–2.

Hynes, J. 2001. *The Lecturer's Tale*. New York: Picador.

Johnson, T. S. 1996. "Deaf Students in Mainstreamed College Composition Courses: Culture and Pedagogy." Diss. Louisiana State University.

Kaufer, D. S., and C. Geisler. 1989. "Novelty in Academic Writing." *Written Communication* 6: 286–311.

Keller, E. Fox, and H. Moglen. 1987. "Competition: A Problem for Academic Women." In *Competition: A Feminist Taboo?*, eds. V. Miner and H. E. Longino, 21–37. New York: The Feminist Press.

Kirsch, G. E. 1993. *Women Writing the Academy: Audience, Authority, and Transformation.* Carbondale: Southern Illinois University Press.

Kraemer, D. 1991. "Abstracting Bodies of/in Academic Discourse." *Rhetoric Review* 10: 52–69.

Kroeber, K. 1993. "Technology and Tribal Narrative." In *Narrative Chance: Postmodern Discourse in Native American Indian Literatures*, ed. G. Vizenor, 17–37. Norman: University of Oklahoma Press.

Kuriloff, P. C. 1996. "What Discourses Have in Common: Teaching the Transaction Between Writer and Reader." *College Composition and Communication* 47: 485–501.

Laurence, D. 1998. "Employment of 1996–97 English Ph.D.s: A Report on the MLA's Census of Ph.D. Placement." *ADE Bulletin* 121: 58–69.

Le Dœuff, M. 1991. *Hipparchia's Choice: An Essay Concerning Women, Philosophy, etc.*, trans. T. Selous. Oxford, UK: Blackwell.

Lincoln, B. 1989. *Discourse and the Construction of Society: Comparative Studies of Myth, Ritual, and Classification.* New York: Oxford University Press.

———. 1991. *Emerging from the Chrysalis: Rituals of Women's Initiation.* New York: Oxford University Press.

Long, M. C., J. H. Holberg, and M. M. Taylor. 1996. "Beyond Apprenticeship: Graduate Students, Professional Development Programs, and the Future(s) of English Studies." *WPA: Writing Program Administration* 20: 66–78.

Longino, H. E. 1987. "The Ideology of Competition." In *Competition: A Feminist Taboo?,* eds. V. Miner and H. E. Longino, 248–58. New York: The Feminist Press.

Lu, M. 1994. "Professing Multiculturalism: The Politics of Style in the Contact Zone." *College Composition and Communication* 45: 442–58.

Lunsford. A. 1992. "Intellectual Property, Concepts of Selfhood, and the Teaching of Writing." *Journal of Basic Writing* 11: 61–73.

Mairs, N. 1994. *Voice Lessons: On Becoming a (Woman) Writer.* Boston: Beacon.

Martin, J. R. 1989. *Reclaiming a Conversation: The Ideal of the Educated Woman.* New Haven: Yale University Press.

Mauch, J. E., and J. W. Birch. 1993. *Guide to the Successful Thesis and Dissertation: A Handbook for Students and Faculty.* 3rd ed. New York: Dekker.

McCarthy, L. P., and S. M. Fishman. 1991. "Boundary Conversations: Conflicting Ways of Knowing in Philosophy and Interdisciplinary Research." *Research in the Teaching of English* 25: 419–68.

McMillan, Gail. 2001. "What to Expect from ETDs: Library Issues and Responsibilities." Paper presented at the Fourth International ETD Conference, California Institute of Technology, Pasadena, March 21–24.

Miller, C. A. 1997. "Better Than What People Told Me I Was: What Students of Color Tell Us About the Multicultural Composition Classroom." In *Writing in Multicultural Settings*, eds. C. Severino, J. Guerra, and J. Butler, 287–97. New York: MLA.

Miller, S. L., B. J. Brueggemann, B. Blue, and D. M. Shepherd. 1997. "Present Perfect and Future Imperfect: Results of a National Survey of Graduate Students in Rhetoric and Composition Programs." *College Composition and Communication* 48: 392–409.

Miller, S. 1991. *Textual Carnivals: The Politics of Composition.* Carbondale: Southern Illinois University Press.

Moffett, J. 1994. "Coming Out Right." In *Taking Stock: The Writing Process Movement in the 90s*, eds. L. Tobin and T. Newkirk, 17–30. Portsmouth, NH: Boynton/Cook.

Moi, T. 1989. "Patriarchal Thought and the Drive for Knowledge." In *Between Feminism and Psychoanalysis*, ed. T. Brennan, 189–205. London: Routledge.

Moore, C. 2000. "A Letter to Women Graduate Students on Mentoring," In *Profession*. 149–56.

Morson, G. S. 1994. *Narrative and Freedom: The Shadows of Time*. New Haven: Yale University Press.

Mortensen, P., and G. E. Kirsch. 1993. "On Authority in the Study of Writing." *College Composition and Communication* 44: 556–72.

Networked Digital Library of Theses and Dissertations. Rev. 2001. http://www.ndltd.org (21 June 2002).

Newkirk, T. 1992. "The Narrative Roots of the Case Study." In *Methods and Methodology in Composition Research*, eds. G. Kirsch and P. Sullivan, 130–52. Carbondale: Southern Illionois University Press.

North, S. 1987. *The Making of Knowledge in Composition: Portrait of an Emerging Field*. Upper Montclair, NJ: Boynton/Cook.

Nuland, S. B. 2001. "The Uncertain Art: Writing." *The American Scholar* 70 (1): 129–32.

Olsen, F. 1999. "Faculty Wariness of Technology Remains a Challenge, Computing Survey Finds." *Chronicle of Higher Education* 29 Oct. 1999. http://chronicle.com/weekly/v46/i10/10a06501.htm (21 June 2002).

Ong, W. J. 1977. *Interfaces of the Word: Studies in the Evolution of Consciousness and Culture*. Ithaca: Cornell University Press.

———. 1981. *Fighting for Life: Contest, Sexuality, and Consciousness*. Ithaca: Cornell University Press.

Pemberton, M. 1993. "Tales Too Terrible to Tell: Unstated Truths and Underpreparation in Graduate Composition Programs." In *Writing Ourselves into the Story: Unheard Voices from Composition Studies*, ed. S. Fontaine and S. Hunter, 154–73. Carbondale: Southern Illinois University Press.

Pirsig, R. M. 1975. *Zen and Art of Motorcycle Maintenance.* New York: Bantam Books.

Pockley, Simon. 1995. *The Flight of Ducks*. Diss. Royal Melbourne Institute of Technology. http://www.acmi.net.au/FOD/ (21 June 2002).

———. 1995, 2001. "Killing the Duck to Keep the Quack: Networked Proliferation and Long-Term Access." http://www.acmi.net.au/FOD/FOD0055.html (21 June 2002).

———. 2001. Personal email. 20 May.

Punch M. 1986. *The Politics and Ethics of Fieldwork*. Beverly Hills, CA: Sage.

Rich, A. 1979. "When We Dead Awaken: Writing as Re-Vision." In *On Lies, Secrets, and Silence*. New York: W.W. Norton.

Rider, J., and E. Broughton. 1994. "Moving Out, Moving Up: Beyond the Basement and Ivory Tower." *JAC* 14: 240–55.

Rilke, R. M. 1972. *Letters to a Young Poet*. New York: Norton.

Robinson, P. 2000. "Within the Matrix: A Hermeneutic Phenomenological Investigation of Student Experiences in Web-Based Computer Conferencing." Diss. Towson University. http://www.towson.edu/~probinso/Dissertation/ (21 June 2002).

———. 2001. Personal email. 21 May.

Rodriguez, R. 1982. *Hunger of Memory: The Education of Richard Rodriguez.* New York: Bantam.

Rosaldo, R. 1999. "A Note on Geertz as a Cultural Essayist." In *The Fate of "Culture": Geertz and Beyond.* Berkeley: University of California Press.

———. 1989. *Culture and Truth*. Boston: Beacon Press.

Rosenthal, R. 1995. "Feminists in Action: How to Practice What We Teach." In *Left Margins: Cultural Studies and Composition Pedagogy,* ed. K. Fitts and A. W. France, 139–55. Albany: SUNY Press.

Said, E. 1974. "An Ethics of Language." *Diacritics* 4: 28–37.

———. 1985. *Beginnings: Intention and Method.* New York: Columbia University Press.

Saltzman, D. 1995. *The Jester Has Lost His Jingle.* Palos Verdes Estates, CA: Jester Company.

Salvatori, M. R., ed. 1996. *Pedagogy: Disturbing History.* Pittsburgh: University of Pittsburgh Press.

Schell, E. E. 1998a. "Who's the Boss?: The Possibilities and Pitfalls of Collaborative Administration for Untenured WPAs." *WPA: Writing Program Administration* 21: 65–80.

——— 1998b. *Gypsy Academics and Mother-Teachers: Gender, Contingent Labor, and Writing Instruction.* Portsmouth, NH: Boynton/Cook.

Scholes, R. 1985. *Textual Power: Literary Theory and the Teaching of English.* New Haven: Yale University Press.

Schweickart, P. P. 1990. "Reading, Teaching, and the Ethic of Care." In *Gender in the Classroom: Power and Pedagogy*, eds. S. L. Gabriel and I. Smithson, 78–95. Chicago: University of Chicago Press.

Shweder, R. A., and E. J. Bourne. 1984. "Does the Concept of the Person Vary Cross-culturally?" In *Culture Theory: Essays on Mind, Self and Emotion,* eds. R. A. Shweder and R. Levin, 158–99. Cambridge: Cambridge University Press.

Smith, R. S. 2000. "Done *Is* Better than Perfect: The Current Crisis in U.S. Higher Education, Its Multiple Consequences, and the Universities' Unwillingness to Fund a Possible Solution." *iMP: The Magazine of Information Impacts.* 7 July 2000. http://www.cisp.org/imp/july_2000/07_00smith.htm (21 June 2002).

Spellmeyer, K. 1998. "Marginal Prospects." *WPA: Writing Program Administration* 21: 162–82.

Sugg, R. 1978. *Motherteacher: The Feminization of American Education.* Charlottesville: University Press of Virginia.

Sullivan, P. A. 1994. "Revising the Myth of the Independent Scholar." In *Writing With: New Directions in Collaborative Teaching, Learning, and Research*, eds. S. Barr Reagan, T. Fox, and D. Bleich, 11–29. Albany: SUNY Press.

Tinto, V. 1993. *Leaving College: Rethinking the Causes and Cures of Student Attrition*. 2nd ed. Chicago: University of Chicago Press.

Tokarczyk, M. M., and E. A. Fay, eds. 1993. *Working-Class Women in the Academy: Laborers in the Knowledge Factory*. Amherst: University of Massachusetts Press.

Torgovnick, M. 1990. "Experimental Critical Writing." *Profession:* 25–27.

Tompkins, J. 1987. "Me and My Shadow." *New Literary History* 19: 169–78.

Trilling, L. 1972. *Sincerity and Authenticity*. Cambridge: Harvard University Press.

Trimbur, J. 2000. "Composition and the Circulation of Writing." *College Composition and Communication* 52: 188–219.

UNESCO. 2001. *The ETD Guide*. http://etdguide.org (21 June 2002).

Urion, M. V. 1998. *Becoming Most Fully Ourselves: Gender, Voice, and Ritual in Dissertations*. Diss. Michigan Technological University. http://sunshine.lib.mtu.edu/ETD/Dissertation/TOC.pdf (21 June 2002).

Veroff, J. "Writing." 1992. In *Surviving Your Dissertation: A Comprehensive Guide to Content and Process*, eds. K. E. Rudestam and R. R. Newton, 145–167. Newbury Park, CA: Sage.

Villanueva, V. 1997. "Whose Voice Is It Anyway? Rodriguez's Speech in Retrospect." In *Living Languages: Contexts for Reading and Writing*, eds. N. Buffinton, M. Diognes, and C. Moneyhun, 109–17. Upper Saddle River, NJ: Prentice Hall.

Walker, J., and T. Taylor. 1998. *The Columbia Guide to Online Style*. New York: Columbia University Press.

———. 2001. "Faces and Interfaces: Teaching Writing in a Technological Age." Plenary address, Research Network Forum, Conference on College Composition and Communication, Denver, March 14–17.

Winterson, J. 1996. *Art [Objects]: Essays on Ecstasy and Effrontery*. New York: Alfred A. Knopf.

Yeats, W. B. 1954. *The Letters of W. B. Yeats*, ed. Allan Wade. London: Hart-Davis.

———. 1959. *Mythologies*. New York: Macmillan.

———. 1964. *Letters on Poetry from W. B. Yeats to Dorothy Wellesley*. London: Oxford.

———. 1965. *Autobiography*. New York: Macmillan.

———. 1992. *Yeats' 'Vision' Papers: The Automatic Script: 25 June 1918 to 29 March 1920,* ed. G. M. Harper, S. L. Adams, B. J. Frieling, and S. L. Sprayberry. Iowa City: University of Iowa Press.

Zawacki, T. M. 1992. "Recomposing as a Woman—An Essay in Different Voices." *College Composition and Communication* 43: 32–9.

Contributors

Fred Arroyo, assistant professor of rhetorical theory and cultural studies at Saint Louis University, teaches a range of courses including ethnic American literacy narratives, composition, and fiction writing. A fiction writer, poet, and interviewer, he is currently at work on *For the Love of My Father* as well as an untitled narrative on literacy, learning, and living.

Sheila L. Carter-Tod, assistant professor of English, teaches composition, linguistics, technical writing, and African American literature at Virginia Polytechnic Institute and State University. Her research interests are language and empowerment in multiple sites, including literacy programs, the study of African American literature, and second-language teaching.

Devan Cook writes poetry and nonfiction, and teaches first-year and advanced composition at Boise State University. Her work is recently published or forthcoming in *TETYC*, *Idaho Writers' Connections*, and *CCC*.

Alys Culhane's personal-pedagogical essays have appeared in *Teaching Writing Creatively*, *The Elements of Alternate Style*, and *Writes of Passage*. From her current residence in Montana, she's at work on a manuscript entitled *Headwinds: The Memoirs of a Cross-Country Bicyclist*, a project she describes as part memoir and part travelogue.

Darrell Fike teaches at Valdosta State University. His work has appeared in various newspapers, literary magazines, scholarly journals, and anthologies, including *Elements of Alternate Style* and *The Subject Is Reading*.

Amy Goodburn is an associate professor of English and women's studies at the University of Nebraska, Lincoln, where she is the composition coordinator. Recent publications include essays in *Composition Studies*, *Concerns*, and in the edited collections *Race, Rhetoric, and Composition*, and *Public Works*. With Deborah Minter she is editing a collection titled *(Re)Presenting Our Practice: Documenting Teaching in Composition Studies.*

Janis E. Haswell teaches writing and British literature at Texas A&M University, Corpus Christi, where she is an associate professor. In addition to articles in *College Composition and Communication*, *Rhetoric Review*, *Yeats Annual*, and elsewhere, she has published monographs on Paul Scott and W. B. Yeats. Her book on Paul Scott's philosophy of place is forthcoming.

Marsha Lee Holmes is an assistant professor in English at Western Carolina University in Cullowhee, North Carolina, where she also directs the first-year composition program. Her work has appeared in the *English Journal*, the *Virginia English Bulletin*, and elsewhere.

Catherine G. Latterell is assistant professor of English at Pennsylvania State University, Altoona College. Her research interests combine composition theory, cultural theory, and critical pedagogy to explore issues in writing programs—particularly the impact of technology on teaching in the humanities.

Carrie Shively Leverenz is associate professor of English and director of composition at Texas Christian University, where she teaches courses in writing, composition theory, and cyberliteracy. For six years she directed the Reading/Writing Center and computer-supported writing classrooms at Florida State University. She is currently working on a book, *Doing the Right Things: Ethical Issues in Institutionalized Writing Instruction.*

Cindy Moore's scholarship focuses on feminist theory and pedagogy, connections between creative and academic writing, and faculty development. Her essays reflecting these interests have appeared in such journals as *Dialogue*, *Feminist Teacher*, *Profession*, and *Readerly/Writerly Texts*. She is an assistant professor and director of composition at St. Cloud State University.

Joseph M. Moxley has recently published his tenth book, *Web of Danger* (a novel). A professor of English at the University of South Florida, he has also published essays in numerous composition journals and is coeditor of such collections as *Creative Writing in America: Theory and Pedagogy* and *Voices & Visions: Refiguring Ethnography in Composition.*

Joy Ritchie is a professor of English and teaches composition, rhetoric, and women's studies courses at the University of Nebraska, Lincoln, where she also directs the Women's Studies Program. With Kate Ronald, she has recently published *Available Means: An Anthology of Women's Rhetoric(s).*

Kate Ronald, Roger and Joyce L. Howe Professor of English at Miami University, teaches courses in composition and rhetoric and works with the School of Business on writing-across-the-curriculum. Her recent collaborations with Hephzibah Roskelly include *Reason to Believe: Romanticism, Pragmatism, and the Teaching of Writing.*

Hephzibah Roskelly teaches composition, rhetoric, and literature at the University of North Carolina, Greensboro, where she is a professor in English and also serves as associate director of women's studies.

Cynthia L. Selfe is a professor of humanities at Michigan Technological University and the founder and coeditor of *Computers and Composition.* The first woman and English teacher to receive an EDUCOM Medal for innovative computer use in higher education, she has also served as the chair of the Conference on College Composition and Communication and of the College section of the National Council of Teachers of English.

Tonya M. Stremalu teaches developmental English, ESL, and English-major courses at Gallaudet University where she is an associate professor. Her primary ongoing scholarly interest concerns literacy and the deaf.

Marilyn Vogler Urion has at various times been a poet, reference librarian, house painter, mother, math teacher—and almost always a student. Since completing her PhD in Michigan Tech's Rhetoric and Technical Communication program, she has worked in graduate school administration. Her interest in gender and the academic community grows out of her experiences on the periphery, including teaching first-year writing for almost a decade as an adjunct.

Janice R. Walker, assistant professor of writing and linguistics at Georgia Southern University, coauthored *The Columbia Guide to Online Style* and is the founder of the Graduate Research Network for the annual Computers and Writing Conference. Her publications include articles on intellectual property, computers, and writing, and electronic theses and dissertations.

Nancy Welch is an associate professor of English at the University of Vermont. Her articles and short stories have appeared in *College English*, *College Composition and Communication*, *Greensboro Review*, *Prairie Schooner*, and elsewhere. Her book *Getting Restless: Rethinking Revision in Writing Instruction* was published by Boynton/Cook.

Peggy Woods is the assistant director of the writing program at the University of Massachusetts, Amherst. As a fiction writer and a compositionist, she has taught creative writing and a range of composition courses. Her fiction has appeared in *The Hawaii Pacific Review*, *Quarter After Eight*, and *13th Moon*.